Fig. 99

Antony Worrall Thompson
REAL FAMILY FOOD

Antony and Jacinta's daughter and friend

Antony Worrall Thompson
REAL FAMILY FOOD

photography by Steve Lee

MITCHELL BEAZLEY

Real Family Food by Antony Worrall Thompson

First published in Great Britain in 2005 by Mitchell Beazley,
an imprint of Octopus Publishing Group Limited,
2–4 Heron Quays, London E14 4JP.
© Octopus Publishing Group Limited 2005
Text © Antony Worrall Thompson 2005

A CIP catalogue record for this book is available from the
British Library.

ISBN 1 84533 125 7

While all reasonable care has been taken during the
preparation of this edition, neither the publisher, editors, nor
the authors can accept responsibility for any consequences
arising from the use thereof or from the information
contained therein.

Commissioning Editor: Rebecca Spry
Executive Art Editor: Yasia Williams-Leedham
Design: Grade Design Consultants
Editor: Susan Fleming
Photography: Steve Lee
Home economy: Sarah Lewis
Food styling: Joanna Harris
Production: Jane Rogers
Index: John Noble

Typeset in Helvetica Neue and Serifa
Printed in Italy

**To the best family in the world – Jacinta, Toby-Jack and
Billie-Lara.**

Acknowledgements
There are so many people to thank but certain individuals or
companies deserve a special mention. Firstly, to the
publishers, Mitchell Beazley and especially Becca Spry, who
has been incredibly patient and very understanding. Thanks
to Yasia Williams and Grade design – the book looks great,
nicely balanced and a terrific design. To Steve Lee and his
team, as always, great photography with inspired styling to
create that family feel. To Jacinta and our two children, Toby-
Jack and Billie-Lara, who inspired me to put this book
together and helped me test recipes, a great family of whom
I'm very proud. To Louise Townsend, my energetic and ultra-
efficient PA, who fielded hundreds of 'phone calls from the
publishers and who was regularly on hand to smooth
troubled waters when the pressures of deadlines occasionally
took their toll. To Fiona Lindsay, Linda Shanks and Lesley
Turnbull at Limelight Management, who are constantly there
to make sure I have more than enough work to handle. To my
teams at Notting Grill, Kew Grill and The Greyhound –
especially David, George, Antonio, Candido, Al and Easer –
who kept the boats afloat during my often extended
absences. To the various friends Nicki, Bridget and Marcus,
Sarah and Jeremy, Catherine and Andrew, and Mike and
Nicky, who acted unknowingly as guinea pigs for many of the
recipes. To Jim, Sophie and Mike for their stoic efforts in the
garden. To Susan Fleming, who skilfully, and with humour,
subbed my writings. To my new family, Maeve and Frank
Shiel, Jacinta's parents, who over the years have guided me
through the trials and tribulations of bringing up the children
– although I get my way when it comes to feeding. And to all
the members of the public who voted me Epson Celebrity Dad
of the Year; I hope this book will help you regain control of
your children, certainly on the food front.

EACH RECIPE IN THE BOOK IS ACCOMPANIED BY A RED, AMBER OR GREEN DOT, INDICATING THE HEALTH QUALITIES OF THE DISH.

RED: Eat one of these dishes no more than once a day. These are treats that tend to be quite high in fat, sugar and/or salt. They should be complemented in your daily diet by plenty of fruit and vegetables and foods that are low in saturated fat, salt and sugar.

AMBER: Eat one of these dishes no more than three times a day. They tend to have a lower proportion of fat, sugar and/or salt than the red dishes and a higher proportion of fruit and vegetables and/or the minerals iron and calcium.

GREEN: Eat these dishes as often as you like as snacks and as meals and try to include at least one of them in your daily diet. They are either a good source of fruit and vegetables or the minerals iron and calcium or both. Try basing your family's diet around these recipes.

Contents

You, your kids and food

You brought your children into the world, their future lies in your hands, and where you lead they will follow. I can make it sound easy, I can make it sound very difficult, but I'm no expert – just a caring dad who has brought four children into this world. My first two, Blake and Sam, didn't get much help from me as their mother left with them when they were two and one. All I could do was provide them with a good education. I would love to have got involved in their food lives as they, just like many others at their age (21 and 19), rely very much on convenience food.

I remember a few years ago, when we were ski-ing in America, making Blake and Sam fresh burgers. They obviously appreciated this gesture as they lapped them up, but their review of my offering made me despair: 'Very good, Dad, but not quite as good as McDonalds!' What's a chef and dad to do? I couldn't believe they had been brainwashed by the marketing power of the Big M. Don't get me wrong, while I wouldn't eat an M myself, I see no problem in children participating in their favourite food on the odd occasion – children must be allowed to be children.

But the world 'children' is the key. They are not adults, certainly for the first part of their lives, and they like to know their parameters – they need guidelines. I think many children are allowed to grow up too fast, and much of this comes from media channels, trendy magazines, TV programmes and the internet. Remember that phrase, 'children must be allowed to be children'. Making them into small adults too early deprives them of all of the wonders of childhood: the fun, the imagination, the fairy tales.

Bring them along slowly. Restrict their access to modern pressures and keeping up with their peers. Shield them from 'labels' by choosing a school with a uniform, and don't be tempted to issue mobile phones too early. Ban the telly during the school week, and introduce them to the wonders of music instead. Read some of the old-fashioned stories to them, join the library or keep them supplied with plenty of books. Make them play outside as much as possible rather than being bedroom-bound with their 'Game Boy' or 'X Box'. Don't fall into the modern habit of letting them stay up late on a regular basis, as sleep is vital for their developing health. I know what you're thinking: 'He's a bit of a tyrant.' But I'd say 'No, I'm just a dad with old-fashioned values, and anyway I haven't finished yet'....

It's all about being a family, non-fragmented, a unit. I'm not completely Victorian in my values – there's no 'children should be seen and not heard' in the AWT household. Quite the opposite. I love my children to express themselves, I want them to converse, to communicate, to be able to have animated conversations with their friends and our adult friends alike.

And how is that skill developed? Around the table, eating good food, discussing their day, the fun, the disappointments. Communication skills won't develop if your children are given a ready meal to devour in front of the telly. Every day we try to sit around the kitchen table for at least one meal; it's so important. Not only is it where conversation begins, it's all about trust. If you eat with your children they will more than likely trust the food and join with you in its enjoyment. It's when you give the children one thing and you eat another that the alarm bells start ringing. I know it is not practical to eat every meal with them, but try and do it as much as possible.

'But how do I get my children to eat their vegetables?' is a question I am frequently asked. It's not easy I grant you, especially if they have become accustomed to ready-meals, takeaways or fast food. You have to be patient, you have to persevere. It takes discipline, a strong will and patience. The key, I'm afraid to say, is telling them what they are going to eat. This may not be what you want to hear and it certainly won't be what the children want to hear, but choice will be your downfall.

We've had it all: the tears, the tantrums. My children are just like any others; they'll try it on and try our patience. My being a chef means very little in their eyes. When we're not looking, vegetables find their way on to the floor 'by mistake'. If the dogs walk over to the table, they've come to realise they're the perfect dustbin for unwanted vegetables. You must be firm, and eventually they will realise that you mean business and that they have to eat their vegetables. The fuss will die down, cabbage will become second nature, and Brussels sprouts may be welcomed!

Remember, you as the parents are the bosses in your own household. Your children expect to follow the house rules and, once they know them, your lives will improve out of all recognition. Your children are in your likeness, they will mimic what you do, so if you enjoy your food – and especially your vegetables – and don't taint them with your dislikes, they will end up as children who eat everything that's put in front of them.

Sounds easy doesn't it, but it isn't, trust me. We had to try everything. We pointed out that people are starving around the world. We showed them the children with dull hair and sunken eyes who get every cold and bug going; we bribed them, we gave them treats – and now, I'm happy to say, we have two happy, healthy children.

There was a time when they would take over an hour to eat their evening meal, hoping I would get bored and remove the plates, but they hadn't taken into account the fact that I'm a Taurean, exceptionally stubborn and love to win, even against the kids. I eventually had to introduce the 20-minute rule: the main meal finished in 20 minutes or they'd have to do chores. We never looked back, meal times became a pleasure, conversation flowed, and the fun was back.

Regain control of your children, they'll live by your rules. Don't give up; persevere, and they'll come round. Make meal times fun, something to look forward to, and worry about manners later. Vary the food you give them: small portions of several foods are much less daunting than large portions of one or two. Don't over-complicate the cooking, Make life easy for yourself. Remember, how you treat them and how you feed them is probably how they will treat their own children, so you really are influencing their futures. Most of all you are building a healthy foundation for your own children to build upon.

'Communication skills won't develop if your children are given a ready-meal to devour in front of the TV'

AWT house rules

Here are some of my house rules. You will, of course, have your own way of doing things, but I thought this might interest you...

Kids must eat their vegetables – no arguments.

Only serve water with meals as juice fills them up.

No salt to be added to food at the table, except to chips.

Wash your hands with soap before and after all meals.

No talking with your mouth full.

No elbows on the table while eating.

One of you to lay the table and one of you to clear away after the meal.

Around the table, tell us something nice you did for someone or something nice someone did for you.

Only give a maximum of two juices a day.

Never walk past the fruit bowl without helping yourself to at least one piece of fruit.

One fizzy drink a day allowed on holiday.

Sweets allowed only once a week.

Muesli for breakfast on Tuesdays and Fridays.

Look after your body, feed it well, and it will serve you well.

Your mother is not your servant; she is someone to love and respect... she likes to hear the words 'yes, Mum'.

Always remember you can't change yesterday, you don't know what tomorrow will bring, so live for today and cherish each person and each moment.

'Look after your body, feed it well, and it will serve you well.'

Breakfasts

Breakfast is a meal that seems to have been consigned to history. With both parents out at work, the last thing you want to do in the morning is cook a healthy start for the kids. There's enough to do without all that – school uniforms to organize, beds to make – on top of which you may be a tad grumpy, so it only takes the slightest thing to set you off. Just putting the kettle on or pouring the milk into a bowl of cereal requires more than enough effort for most people.

And yet, if you deny your children a proper start to the day, you can seriously damage their ability to concentrate on their lessons at school. Our bodies need a kick-start, we need fuel to fire up the engine, we need brain food, and we need enough of it to keep us going until lunchtime. To create a smooth start to the day, a little planning is all it takes.

It is not good enough just to put out the cereal the night before and let the children help themselves to milk from the fridge. Too many cereals are like little time-bombs: packed full of sugar and salt, they increase sugar dependency, some having as much as the equivalent of 10-14 teaspoons of sugar in the average portion. So what happens to a child's body not yet developed enough to cope with such sugar rushes? The blood sugar levels go shooting skywards, the child becomes hyperactive and then, by 10.30-11 in the morning, sugar levels come crashing down again and lethargy sets in, along with lack of concentration and tiredness. To counteract this they require a snack, usually a sweet cereal bar, and the vicious spiral continues.

Preparing fresh breakfasts may sound easier said than done – and I know where you're coming from – but that little bit of effort will make you and your kids' day so much better. Remember, it's also another occasion when you can all get round the kitchen table and communicate. Being together, with you eating the same food as the children, all helps to build that bond between parents and their kids and sets everyone up for the day.

'Some breakfast cereals have as much as the equivalent of 10-14 teaspoons of sugar in the average portion.'

Banana porridge with caramelized peaches

Porridge is a great way to start the day, fighting off the mid-morning hunger pangs, as it's a low GI (glycaemic index) food, slowly releasing energy into the bloodstream.

Serves 4

600ml (1 pint) semi-skimmed milk, simmering
200g (7oz) porridge oats
a pinch of salt
a pinch of ground cinnamon
4 tbsp dark muscovado sugar
2 ripe bananas, peeled
25g (1oz) unsalted butter
2 ripe peaches, stoned and each cut into 8 wedges
2 tbsp caster sugar

1 Into the simmering milk, pour the porridge oats with the salt and cinnamon, and stir over a low heat for 5 minutes.

2 Mash the soft brown sugar into the bananas, creating a textured purée. Fold this into the porridge, and cook for a further 5 minutes.

3 Meanwhile, heat the butter in a frying pan. Add the peaches and brown on both sides, then add the caster sugar and cook gently until the peaches are soft and golden.

4 Divide the porridge between 4 warm bowls and scatter the peaches on top.

Also try

- Use caramelized apples or pears instead of peaches.

Kipper toast

A delicious breakfast, and a great way of getting children to eat a portion of oily fish.

Serves 4

4 kipper fillets, cooked and skinned

115g (4oz) unsalted butter, softened

¼ tsp cayenne pepper

⅛ tsp freshly grated nutmeg

100ml (3½ fl oz) double cream

85g (3oz) Cheddar cheese, grated

4 slices country bread

4 tbsp mango chutney

1 Mash the kipper fillets with the butter, cayenne pepper, nutmeg, double cream and Cheddar cheese.

2 Toast the bread slices on one side only. Spread the untoasted side with the mango chutney, then top with the kipper mix.

3 Pop the toasts, topping side up, under the grill until hot and bubbling.

Also try

- Use smoked salmon, smoked mackerel or cooked smoked haddock instead of kippers.

- Leave the Cheddar cheese out of the mix and sprinkle it on top before grilling.

- Adults may prefer a smear of creamed horseradish instead of mango chutney.

Croque Monsieur

There's nothing wrong with a good toastie from time to time, and the beauty of this classic French sandwich is the base mix, which can be made well in advance and kept in the fridge for at least a week. Double or treble the mix and keep well wrapped so you're always ready for an instant toasted sandwich.

Serves 4

55g (2oz) unsalted butter
1 tbsp plain flour
175ml (6fl oz) semi-skimmed milk
1 tsp Dijon mustard
1 free-range egg yolk
salt and ground black pepper
a pinch of freshly grated nutmeg
8 slices white bread
4 slices cooked ham
115g (4oz) Gruyère cheese, grated

1 Melt 20g (¾oz) of the butter in a saucepan, add the flour and stir over a low heat for 3 minutes.

2 Slowly add the milk, whisking constantly. Leave to simmer until the mixture has thickened and reduced by about a third. Remove from the heat and stir in the mustard and egg yolk. Season with salt, pepper and nutmeg, and leave to cool completely.

3 Place half the bread slices on a baking tray. Top each piece of bread with a slice of ham, then with some of the sauce, then Gruyère and finally with another piece of bread.

4 Melt half the remaining butter in a large frying pan and fry the sandwiches on both sides until golden, adding the remaining butter when you need it.

5 Cut each sandwich in half to serve.

Also try

- Top each sandwich with a fried egg for a Croque Madame.

- Omit the ham and replace with sliced tomatoes.

- If you are not into fried food, simply toast the sandwich under the grill.

Eggy bread pockets stuffed with crispy bacon and apples

Eggy bread, French toast or pain perdu all constitute roughly the same dish, a breakfast favourite for many a family. This version provides a very substantial breakfast, with plenty of energy and plenty of brain food.

Serves 4

8 rashers smoked streaky bacon
3 Granny Smith apples, peeled, cored and each cut into 8 wedges
juice and zest of 1 unwaxed lemon
150ml (5fl oz) water
115g (4oz) caster sugar
150ml (5fl oz) semi-skimmed milk
150ml (5fl oz) single cream
4 free-range eggs, beaten
1 tsp vanilla extract
½ tsp ground cinnamon
4 thick slices country bread or brioche (1-2 days old)
55g (2oz) unsalted butter, melted

To serve
maple syrup
Greek yoghurt

1 Preheat the oven to 170°C/325°F/gas mark 3. Place the bacon on a rack on a roasting tray in the oven and cook until golden, about 10-15 minutes. The bacon will crisp when you remove it from the oven.

2 Meanwhile, toss the apple wedges in the lemon juice and zest, then place in a saucepan with the water and half the sugar. Cook over a medium heat until the apples have softened but are still holding their shape. Drain and set aside. Retain the apple cooking liquor.

3 Beat together the milk, cream, eggs, vanilla, cinnamon and remaining sugar, and set aside. Add the retained apple poaching liquor to the mix.

4 Slit open one side of each slice of bread, creating a pocket. Stuff each pocket with 2 slices bacon and 6 slices apple. Place the 4 bread pockets in a shallow tray and pour over the eggy-cream. Allow the pockets to soak up the mixture for 2 minutes.

5 Heat the butter in a frying pan. Carefully lift the bread pockets from the mixture into the pan: you might need to do this one at a time. Cook the pockets for 2 minutes on each side, until golden. Remove from the pan and place on the bacon rack, one at a time. Cook in the preheated oven for 10 minutes. Serve immediately with a drizzle of maple syrup and a dollop of yoghurt.

Also try

- Use uncooked slices of tomato or pre-cooked field mushrooms instead of the apples, and leave out the poaching liquor.

Citrus hot cakes with warm strawberries

A lovely weekend brunch that works as a pud as well. You can have fun by adding other fruit or vegetable juices instead of citrus.

Serves 4

175ml (6fl oz) semi-skimmed milk
3 free-range eggs, separated
grated zest and juice of 1
  unwaxed orange
1 tbsp lemon juice
1 tsp orange-blossom water
  (optional)
25g (1oz) unsalted butter, melted
200g (7oz) plain flour, sifted
1½ tsp baking powder
4 tbsp caster sugar
25g (1oz) dried strawberry pieces
  or dried cranberries
vegetable oil or extra melted
  butter

Warm strawberries
225g (8oz) strawberries, hulled
  and halved
1 tsp vanilla extract
2 tbsp runny honey

1   Combine the milk with the egg yolks, citrus zest and juices, orange-blossom water if using, and melted butter.

2   In a separate bowl, combine the flour, baking powder, half the caster sugar and the dried strawberry pieces. Slowly whisk in the milk mixture until just combined.

3   Beat the egg whites to soft peaks, then fold in the remaining sugar and continue to beat until stiff and glossy. Fold a spoon of the egg whites into the batter to slacken the mix, then fold in the remainder until well combined.

4   Spray a non-stick pan with vegetable oil or brush lightly with melted butter, and place over a moderate heat. Drop 2 tbsp of the mixture into the pan; depending on the size of the pan, only cook 2-3 at once. Cook until little bubbles start to appear on the surface of each hot cake, about 2 minutes, then flip over and cook until golden, about 2 more minutes. Keep warm while cooking the remainder.

5   Meanwhile, place all the ingredients for the strawberries in a saucepan over a moderate heat. Stirring regularly, cook until the strawberries are warm and have released some of their juices.

6   To serve, place 2 or 3 hot cakes on 4 warm plates and top with the warm strawberries.

Also try

Instead of the strawberry mixture, try:
- halved figs, grilled

- very thin slices of pineapple

- a salad of oranges and mint.

Crumpets with raspberry ripple yoghurt

Crumpets are usually seen as a tea-time thing, but they make a great alternative energy-giving carbohydrate to the popular toast at breakfast.

Serves 4

225g (8oz) raspberries
juice of 2 limes
2 tbsp icing sugar
250g (9oz) Greek yoghurt
4-8 crumpets
2 tbsp raspberry jam

1   Blend half the raspberries in a liquidizer with the lime juice and icing sugar until smooth. Pass the purée through a fine sieve to remove the pips.

2   Lightly crush the remaining raspberries with the back of a spoon and fold into the raspberry purée.

3   For the next stage, get one of the children to help. One of you stir the yoghurt into a bowl while the other pours half of the raspberry mix in so that you obtain a swirl or ripple effect. Don't overwork, otherwise it will be just a raspberry-pink yoghurt. This takes a bit of practice!

4   Meanwhile, toast the crumpets and, while still hot, spread each with a little raspberry jam. Place on a warm plate and immediately put a dollop of the ripple yoghurt on top. Spoon the remaining raspberry purée around the crumpets.

Also try

- Use strawberries or blackberries in the purée instead of raspberries and serve with their relevant jams.

- Spread the crumpets with honey instead of jam.

- Fold chopped nuts into the yoghurt before adding the purée.

- Top the crumpets with yoghurt combined with apple sauce, then caramelized apples (see page 12).

Slow-release energy ideas

I know it's a bit anal, but we try and plan our children's breakfast week, as variety appeals to them. We concentrate on slow-release energy foods such as muesli or porridge, although certainly not every day. Many mueslis have too much sugar or contain a seed or a nut that the children don't like, so the simple answer is to make your own. 'You're having a laugh,' I hear you say. But it really is as simple as popping into a health-food store or some of the better supermarkets and picking up a few packets. A whole host of dried fruits, nuts, seeds and grains are available to combine, and to start with you can mix some of the children's favourite cereal with the muesli, slowly weaning them off it. Try and concentrate on products with natural sugars rather than added ones.

On another day, we might give the kids a fresh fruit salad with yoghurt. Try not to buy sweetened fruit yoghurts, as it's so easy to make your own. Give them something like natural yoghurt with fresh berries and a little honey – they'll love it. On a couple of days a week porridge features, but please don't use those instant highly sweetened porridge purée substitutes. You need the slow-release energy features of proper porridge. It'll take 5 minutes to cook – hardly a large effort first thing in the morning – and it'll give the children energy right through until lunchtime, with no need for a sweet mid-morning break. Try my banana porridge on page 12.

Eggs should feature a couple of times a week. Being a whole food, they provide healthy nutrients. Give me a couple of eggs and I'll have breakfast on the table within 5 minutes, whether it be boiled eggs and soldiers, an omelette, scrambled or occasionally fried with another brain food, bacon. You can save yourself even more time by serving poached eggs on toast because you can poach them the night before. Just fill the saucepan with about 10cm (4 inches) water, add 1 tbsp of vinegar per litre of water, and bring to the boil. Crack the eggs into the roll of the boil, reduce the heat and cook for 2½ minutes; lift out, plunge into iced water and pop into the fridge. The next morning, when making the tea or coffee and putting on the toast, just remove the eggs from the iced water and pour over boiling water from the kettle. Leave for 45 seconds and you'll have perfect soft eggs ready to pop on to your buttered toast.

'Concentrate on products with natural sugars rather than added ones.'

Passion fruit smoothie

A great way of taking your vitamins.
Drink or pour over your cereal.

Serves 2

2 passion fruits, pulp and seeds
   only
1 tbsp runny honey
1 tbsp lime juice
1 kiwi, peeled and cut into
   chunks
1 tbsp wheatgerm
150ml (5fl oz) fresh orange juice
150ml (5fl oz) semi-skimmed milk
150g (5½oz) Greek yoghurt
6 tbsp crushed ice

1   Place all the ingredients in a liquidizer and blend for
1 minute, until smooth.

2   Pour into 2 glasses. If the smoothie is too thick, add extra
milk or orange juice.

Mango smoothie

Serves 2

1 ripe mango, peeled, stoned and
   roughly diced
150g (5½oz) strawberries, hulled,
   or raspberries
1 banana, peeled and sliced
1 tbsp runny honey
300ml (10fl oz) semi-skimmed
   milk
6 tbsp crushed ice

1   Place the mango pieces and strawberries in a liquidizer and
blend until smooth.

2   Add the banana, honey and milk and blend until smooth
with the crushed ice. Pour into 2 glasses.

Dried fruit compote

Something to make in advance and store in a Kilner jar in the fridge...a healthy start to the day.

Serves 6

115g (4oz) dried apricots
55g (2oz) dried cherries
55g (2oz) dried blueberries
55g (2oz) dried figs
55g (2oz) dried pears
55g (2oz) dried mango
½ cinnamon stick
2 tbsp runny honey
2 cloves
½ vanilla pod, split
finely grated zest of ½ unwaxed
   lemon
a pinch of saffron threads, soaked
   in 2 tbsp hot water
15g (½oz) flaked almonds, toasted
15g (½oz) pine nuts
a few drops of orange-blossom
   water or rosewater (optional)

To serve
cereal or wheatgerm
Greek yoghurt

1   Place all the ingredients up to and including the saffron water in a non-reactive saucepan and just cover with cold water. Bring to the boil, reduce the heat, cover and simmer for 25 minutes. Top up with water if necessary.

2   Allow to cool, then add the remaining ingredients and stir. Remove the cinnamon stick, vanilla pod and cloves.

3   Serve with some cereal and/or wheatgerm and a dollop of Greek yoghurt.

Also try

- The combination of dried fruits is down to you. A popular combo is prunes, dried apples and apricots.

- Once you add muesli to the mix you get a lovely crunch added to the perfume of the dried fruits.

Ricotta griddle cakes with honeyed yoghurt and berries

A winner from the USA, loved by children and adults alike, perfect for brunch food.

Makes 12

325g (11½oz) ricotta cheese

175ml (6fl oz) semi-skimmed milk

1 tbsp runny honey

4 free-range eggs, separated

225g (8oz) plain flour

1 tsp baking powder

2 tbsp caster sugar

2 tbsp vegetable oil or melted
  butter

Honeyed yoghurt and berries

200g (7oz) tub Greek yoghurt

1 tsp ground cinnamon (optional)

3 tbsp runny honey

325g (11½oz) mixed berries
  (raspberries, cut strawberries,
  blueberries)

1   For the griddle cakes, combine the first 3 ingredients with the egg yolks, and beat until smooth. Retain the egg whites.

2   Combine the flour and baking powder, then sift into the ricotta mix and fold together to combine.

3   Beat the egg whites to soft peaks in a very clean bowl, then fold in the caster sugar and beat until stiff and glossy. Add a spoonful of the egg whites to the ricotta mix to slacken it, then fold in the remainder of the egg whites.

4   Oil or butter a non-stick frying pan and spoon 2 tbsp of the ricotta batter into the pan for each griddle cake. Don't overcrowd the pan. Cook over a medium-to-low heat for about 2 minutes before flipping them over and repeating until golden. Cook in batches and keep warm.

5   Meanwhile, combine the yoghurt with the cinnamon and 2 tbsp of honey.

6   Spoon the yoghurt over the cakes, top with the berries, and drizzle with the remaining honey.

Also try

- Caramelized apples.

- Brown-sugar bananas (see page 12).

- Crisp bacon and maple syrup.

- Oven-roasted tomatoes

Overnight apple muesli

I learnt a version of this dish from Ballymaloe House, near Cork in Ireland. In most countries in Europe they soak their muesli overnight to soften it; we in the UK seem to be one of the few countries that eat muesli crunchy with a little milk.

Serves 4

325g (11½oz) rolled oats
300ml (10fl oz) apple juice
2 Granny Smith apples, cored and
   grated
200g (7oz) Greek yoghurt
55g (2oz) sultanas or other dried
   fruit
25g (1oz) flaked almonds, toasted
2 tbsp runny honey

1   Soak the oats in the apple juice overnight or for at least 1 hour.

2   Just prior to eating, fold in the grated apples, yoghurt, sultanas and almonds.

3   Divide between 4 bowls and drizzle with honey.

Apple zing

Health in a glass – but you need a centrifugal juicer for this one.

Serves 2

3 apples or pears, unpeeled
1 celery stick
2 carrots, peeled
1 x 50p thickness piece peeled
   fresh root ginger

1   Process all the ingredients in a centrifrugal juicer.

2   Serve immediately in 2 glasses.

Wholemeal soda bread

Everyone should be able to make at least one loaf of bread, so this is the one. No proving, no kneading, pure simplicity and the children will love to get involved.

Makes 2 loaves

900ml (1½ pints) semi-skimmed milk
juice of 2 lemons
550g (1¼lb) wholemeal stone-ground flour
550g (1¼lb) plain white flour
2 level tsp salt
2 rounded tsp bicarbonate of soda

1   Preheat the oven to 230°C/450°F/gas mark 8. To sour the milk, pour it into a large jug with the lemon juice. Allow it to stand for 15 minutes to thicken and separate before stirring.

2   Sift the dry ingredients together into a large bowl, tipping any bran left in the sieve into the bowl. Make a well in the centre and into that pour 750ml (26fl oz) of the soured milk.

3   Flour your hands. Working from the centre, combine the mixture with either your hand or a wooden spoon, adding more of the soured milk if necessary. The dough should be soft, but not sticky. If it does become too sticky, simply add a little more flour.

4   Turn out on to a floured board and knead lightly before cutting the dough into two. Shape into two round loaves, flatten slightly to about 5cm (2 inches) thick and place on to a flat, floured baking sheet.

5   Using a large floured knife, mark a very deep cross in each loaf and dust the tops with the flour. Bake in the preheated oven for 15-20 minutes, then reduce the heat to 200°C/400°F/gas mark 6 and bake for another for 20-25 minutes, or until the bread is cooked and the loaves sound hollow when tapped.

6   Allow to cool on a rack. The bread freezes well.

Also try

- These rustic loaves take all sorts of extras: different seeds, dried fruits and nuts, apricot and spinach, crispy bacon and seaweed, or crushed pork scratchings can be added with the dry ingredients.

- Use prepared buttermilk instead of souring your own milk.

Lunches

At weekends it's great to get the whole family round the table to eat lunch. If your children will be burning off calories through activities and sport in the afternoon, they'll need to eat enough carbohydrate at lunchtime to keep them going, so they should have a substantial meal with plenty of pasta, rice, bread or potatoes. On more relaxed days, when little exercise is planned for the afternoon, a light soup or salad will suffice – and you'll find a number of examples of those in this chapter too.

It's important to allow children to be children, and kids love foods such as pizzas, sausages and pies. But if you can come up with versions of these dishes that are slightly healthier than the norm, perhaps a pie with a lid of mashed potato rather than pastry, you can encourage them to eat more healthily while giving them the kind of food they like.

If you're planning a pudding at lunchtime, try to stick to simple fruit except for on the most active days. Sugary foods must be the bane of most parents' lives. Kids love sweet things, and this taste can last well into adulthood and sometimes for the rest of our lives. Yet sugar is one of the few foods that gives no benefits to the body's nutrition; it is unnecessary. Certainly it gives you energy, but then so does any carbohydrate. It's far better to get your energy from non-added sugar that is found in natural foods. Fruit and plenty of vegetables contain natural sugar.

Children today eat too many sugary foods – not just sweets, but also cereals, fruit juices and processed foods, including ready-meals. In our house we ban fizzy drinks except at parties and we only allow one or two juices a day, two on holidays. So I'd recommend only giving water with lunch – and indeed with any other meal.

The other thing to consider is that you probably won't want to spend too long in the kitchen preparing lunch, so try to stick to simple recipes, leaving you plenty of time to have fun as a family.

'Get your energy from non-added sugar. Fruit and plenty of vegetables contain natural sugar.'

Spaghetti with fresh tomato sauce and a herby breadcrumb crunch

I don't know a child who doesn't love pasta. This dish is a little different as it introduces them to the vibrant taste of fresh tomatoes and they'll just love the crunchy topping.

Serves 4

300g (10½oz) spaghetti
salt and ground black pepper
6 ripe plum tomatoes, roughly
    chopped
1 small red onion, finely chopped
6 basil leaves, ripped small
90ml (3fl oz) extra virgin olive oil

Breadcrumbs
2 garlic cloves
1 tbsp soft thyme leaves
2 tsp rosemary leaves
2 tbsp flat-leaf parsley leaves
150ml (5fl oz) extra virgin olive oil
1 x 2-day-old small ciabatta loaf,
    broken into small chunks

1   For the breadcrumb topping, blend the garlic and herbs in a food processor until finely chopped. You may need to add a splash of the oil. Scrape the bowl down from time to time, then add the bread and process into rough crumbs.

2   Heat the remaining olive oil for the breadcrumbs in a frying pan, then add the herby crumbs and cook for 4-5 minutes over a medium heat until golden and crunchy, stirring continuously. Drain on kitchen paper and keep warm. These breadcrumbs will store for 3 days in an airtight container.

3   Cook the spaghetti in a deep pan of boiling salted water according to the pack instructions until *al dente*. You will need to stir the pasta for the first couple of minutes to stop it sticking. Drain and return to the pan, leaving a small residue of water clinging to the pasta.

4   Meanwhile, combine the tomatoes, onion, basil and olive oil, and season to taste. Add this cold sauce to the pasta and toss to combine. Tip into bowls and sprinkle with the crisp breadcrumbs. Serve immediately.

Also try

● If your children are not fond of raw tomatoes, here's a quick cooked tomato sauce. Sweat 1 finely chopped onion in 1 tbsp olive oil with 2 crushed garlic cloves for 8 minutes. Add 1 x 400g can chopped tomatoes, 85g (3oz) chopped sun-dried tomatoes and 12 oregano leaves. Bring to the boil then reduce the heat and simmer for 10 minutes, until thickened. If desired, fold in 2 tsp pesto before serving and offer plenty of freshly grated Parmesan.

A version of spaghetti carbonara

An all-time favourite, the egg and bacon pasta, which is often abused to make a complete hash! I do mine traditionally without the use of cream, but that decision should be yours.

Serves 4

400g (14oz) best-quality dried
  spaghetti
salt and ground black pepper
50ml (2fl oz) good olive oil
25g (1oz) unsalted butter
225g (8oz) pancetta or smoked
  streaky bacon, cut into 1cm
  (½ inch) lardons
1 onion, finely diced
2 garlic cloves, crushed to a paste
  with a little salt
2 free-range eggs and 2 egg yolks
55g (2oz) Parmesan cheese,
  freshly grated

1 Bring a large saucepan of salted water to the boil and at the same time heat a large frying pan over a medium heat. Grab the spaghetti in one fistful and place it vertically in the water. As it softens, push it further into the water until the pan will take it all. Stir for the first 3 minutes to stop it sticking together.

2 At the same time, heat the oil and butter in the frying pan until foaming, add the pancetta or bacon and cook over a medium heat for 3 minutes, until it has a nice golden colour. Add the onion and garlic and cook for 6-7 minutes, until slightly softened and with a little colour.

3 Meanwhile, beat the eggs and egg yolks in a bowl large enough to take the pasta, then fold in the Parmesan and a few turns of black pepper.

4 Drain the pasta in a colander and, with water still clinging to the pasta, tip it on to the eggs and cheese. Immediately fold together so that the heat of the pasta and its clinging water combine to cook the eggs and produce a creamy emulsion.

5 Fold in the crispy bacon mixture and stir well to combine. Serve immediately with a topping of extra grated Parmesan.

Also try

- Hide vegetables in the pasta: peas, spinach and/or small broccoli florets or chopped tomato.

- Add a few cubes of mozzarella; children love its stringy quality.

- Whisk 150ml (5fl oz) double cream or reduced-fat Greek yoghurt into the eggs before adding the pasta.

Mainstay mince

With all the problems associated with beef, mince has slipped out of favour, which is silly as beef is now probably safer than it's been for 20 years. This is a good standby for making into lots of dishes (see below), so make large amounts and freeze.

Serves 12 (good for freezing)

115g (4oz) streaky bacon, diced
150ml (5fl oz) olive oil
2 onions, finely diced
2 celery sticks, finely diced
2 carrots, finely diced
5 garlic cloves, crushed with a
little salt
2 tsp soft thyme leaves
2 bay leaves
2 tsp dried oregano
2 x 400g cans chopped tomatoes
2 tbsp tomato purée
2 tbsp anchovy essence
2 tbsp Worcestershire sauce
1.8kg (4lb) minced beef
225g (8oz) fresh chicken livers,
finely chopped
1 x 750ml bottle dry red wine
(optional)
up to 2.25 litres (4 pints) chicken,
beef or lamb stock
salt and ground black pepper

1 In a large heavy-based saucepan, fry the bacon in 2 tbsp olive oil. When the bacon is crisp and has released some fat, add the onions, celery, carrot, garlic, thyme, bay and oregano, and cook over a medium heat until they have softened.

2 Add the canned tomatoes, tomato purée, anchovy essence and Worcestershire sauce, stir and continue to cook.

3 Meanwhile, in a large frying pan, heat a little olive oil and fry the mince in small batches until browned. Break up any lumps with the back of a wooden spoon. Repeat until all the meat is used up. After each batch, add the meat to the sauce.

4 In the same frying pan, fry the chicken livers in a little more olive oil until browned all over, then add to the meat.

5 Deglaze the frying pan with some red wine, if using, scraping any crusty bits off the bottom. Pour this wine, the remaining wine and enough stock to cover the meat into the saucepan. Bring to the boil, reduce the heat and simmer, stirring from time to time, for about 2 hours. Season to taste. If the liquid reduces too much, top up with water or stock.

6 When the meat is tender, allow to cool, then refrigerate. Lift off the solidified fat and discard. Freeze in small batches.

Also try

- Mince usually comes from very tough cuts of beef, so shouldn't be cooked in a hurry. If you're in a rush, use minced lamb, but reduce the stock and wine by half and only cook for 45 minutes.

- This base can be converted into bolognese, moussaka, cannelloni, lasagne, shepherd's pie and fillings for jacket potatoes.

Ricotta, tomato and chorizo puff pastry pizza

Ready-made puff pastry makes a good alternative to a normal bread-based pizza or ready-made pizza bases that tend to be thick and stodgy.

Serves 2-4

2 x 23cm (9 inch) discs puff pastry, rolled 1cm (½ inch) thick

325g (11½oz) ricotta cheese or cream cheese

90ml (3fl oz) double cream

1 tbsp pesto (optional)

2 free-range eggs, beaten

55g (2oz) Parmesan cheese, freshly grated

125g (4½oz) ball mozzarella, drained and diced

1 tbsp snipped chives

salt and ground black pepper

175g (6oz) uncooked (if possible) chorizo, cut into 5mm (¼ inch) slices

4 ripe tomatoes, cut into 5mm (¼ inch) slices

1 free-range egg yolk, beaten

1 Preheat the oven to 220°C/425°F/gas mark 7. Place the puff pastry discs on lightly floured baking sheets.

2 Combine the ricotta with the cream, pesto, eggs, Parmesan and mozzarella. Beat well to combine, then fold in the chives and seasoning. Spoon this mixture on to the pastry, leaving a 1cm (½ inch) border all around the edge.

3 Starting in the centre, alternating between the chorizo and tomatoes, arrange a pin-wheel design of the 2 ingredients on top of the filling on both pizzas.

4 Brush the edge of the pizzas with the egg yolk, then place the baking trays in the preheated oven. Cook for 10 minutes, then reduce the heat to 190°C/375°F/gas mark 5 and cook for a further 20 minutes, until they are bubbling and golden.

5 Serve immediately with a leaf salad if you're brave enough. These pizzas are also excellent served at room temperature.

Also try

- Try a little camouflage by folding some chopped cooked spinach into the cream cheese mix.

- You could use small chunks of fresh salmon instead of chorizo.

- If the children are not ready for chorizo, some slices of uncooked pork sausages are very acceptable – they'll cook on the pizza.

Mini beef pies

Served hot or cold, these mini pies are always popular, especially with some mash and a few pickles on the side.

Serves 6

450g (1lb) mainstay mince (see page 33)
115g (4oz) frozen peas, defrosted
3 sheets ready-rolled puff pastry
2 tbsp tomato ketchup (optional)
1 free-range egg, lightly beaten

1 Combine the mince with the peas and set aside.

2 Cut 2 circles of approximately 13cm (5 inches) in diameter from opposite corners of each sheet of puff pastry. Cut 2 circles of approximately 9cm (3½ inches) in diameter from the remaining corners of each sheet of pastry. Place the larger circles in 6 holes of a large non-stick muffin tray to cover the base and sides; trim off any excess pastry. Prick the bottoms of each pastry case and cover with baking paper. Refrigerate, along with the small circles, for half an hour.

3 Preheat the oven to 190°C/375°F/gas mark 5.

4 Fill each lined pastry case with uncooked rice or baking beans and bake in the preheated oven for 12 minutes. Remove the baking paper and rice or beans and allow the pastry to cool.

5 Spoon the mince and peas into the cooked cases. Top each with a little ketchup, if using. Brush the edges of the pastry with a little of the beaten egg. Top the filled pies with the smaller pastry circles, pressing the edges together to seal. Brush the tops with the remaining beaten egg.

6 Bake the pies in the preheated oven for 20–25 minutes, until puffed and golden. Serve hot with buttery mash.

Also try

- Fold in baked beans instead of peas.

Sweet and sour sausages and mash

Children for the most part love sausage and mash, but they also love sweet and sour pork at the local Chinese, so why not combine the two?

Serves 4

8 of your favourite pork sausages

8 rashers rindless dry-cured bacon

2 tsp vegetable oil

8 slices Emmental or Gruyère cheese

Sauce

150ml (5fl oz) Heinz tomato ketchup

75ml (2½fl oz) cider vinegar

½ onion, finely chopped

3 tbsp dark muscovado sugar

2 tsp English mustard

Mash

1kg (2¼lb) floury potatoes, peeled, washed and cut into 2.5cm (1 inch) chunks

salt and ground white pepper

85g (3oz) unsalted butter

225ml (8fl oz) warm semi-skimmed milk

1 Preheat the oven to 190°C/375°F/gas mark 5. Place the sausages in a preheated frying pan and cook them quickly until brown all over but not cooked through. Allow to cool.

2 Combine all the sauce ingredients and heat until the sugar has melted and the onions have softened, about 12 minutes.

3 Make a deep incision the length of each sausage but not right through, and drizzle some sauce into it. Wrap each sausage in a bacon rasher to bring it back to its shape. Oil a baking dish and put the sausages side by side in it. Cover the sausages with the cheese, then drizzle with the remaining sauce. Cook in the preheated oven for 20 minutes.

4 Meanwhile, make the mash by simmering the potatoes in salted water for 12-15 minutes. Drain, then put the colander over the pan on a low heat for 2 minutes to dry the potatoes.

5 Return the potatoes to the saucepan with a pinch of salt and ground white pepper and mash until smooth. Fold in the butter and warm milk and beat until combined. Check the seasoning.

6 Place a dollop of mash on 4 warm plates and top with 2 cheesy sausages. Drizzle with any cooking juices.

Also try

- Place the sausages on a bed of baked beans or fried onions before cooking in the oven.

- Add mango chutney or Branston pickle instead of sweet and sour sauce to the centre of the sausage.

- Fold some roast garlic purée or grated cheese into the mashed potato while it is still hot.

Cottage pies in baked potatoes

This is a fun way to serve cottage pie. A few buttered peas are all that is needed.

Serves 4

4 large jacket potatoes, washed
85g (3oz) unsalted butter
salt and ground black pepper
85g (3oz) Boursin herb and garlic
  cheese
450g (1lb) mainstay mince (see
  page 33)

1   Preheat the oven to 200°C/400°F/gas mark 6.

2   Push a metal skewer through the centre of each potato: this reduces the cooking time and allows the steam to escape. Pop them into the preheated oven on a rack rather than in a baking dish and bake for about 1 hour, or until the potatoes feel soft when squeezed.

3   Remove a shallow lid from the top of each potato, scoop out the flesh into a bowl and mash with the butter, salt and pepper and Boursin cheese. Fill the cavities half full with the mince mix and pipe or spoon the potato back on top. Fluff up with a fork.

4   Return to the oven and bake until the potato is golden and the mince is hot, about 20 minutes. Serve with a green vegetable or a well-dressed leaf salad.

Also try

- Leave out the herb cheese and sprinkle the top with grated Cheddar or Emmental cheese instead.

The really useful chicken recipe

This poached chicken recipe has a myriad of uses: chicken curries, sandwiches, salads or just as it is, served with a soy dip.

Serves 6

1 x 1.6kg (3½lb) free-range chicken
4 spring onions, sliced
5 x 50p thickness discs fresh root ginger
6 garlic cloves
2 hot dried chillies
1 tbsp sea salt
10 black peppercorns
2 tbsp vegetable oil

1   Place the chicken in a tightly fitting saucepan, cover with water and add all the remaining ingredients, apart from the oil.

2   Bring to the boil and simmer for 20 minutes, turning the chicken once during the cooking process. Cover with a lid and switch off the heat. Allow the chicken to relax in the liquor for 2 hours. Check it is cooked through.

3   Remove the chicken, then rub all over with oil. Allow to cool completely, then cut up and use as required.

Also try

- Use the cooking liquid as a stock for the soup on page 41.

Chicken, sweetcorn and noodle soup

A light and healthy soup that makes good use of the stock from the clean and green chicken salad on page 45.

Serves 4

1.2 litres (2 pints) chicken stock (see page 45)

175g (6oz) sweetcorn kernels, fresh or frozen

115g (4oz) sugar-snap peas, topped and tailed

4 spring onions, cut thinly on the diagonal

325g (11½oz) cooked free-range chicken, shredded

2 tsp sesame oil

85g (3oz) thin Chinese egg noodles, cooked, refreshed and drained

2 tbsp light soy sauce

2 tsp liquid honey

juice of 1 lime

2 mild red chillies, seeded and very thinly sliced

1 small handful coriander leaves

8 mint leaves, shredded

1 handful baby spinach leaves

1 Place the stock and sweetcorn in a saucepan, bring to the boil, and simmer for 8 minutes.

2 Add the sugar-snap peas and spring onions and cook for a further 2 minutes.

3 Add the remaining ingredients, bring back to the boil and cook for a further minute, or until the spinach has wilted. Check the seasoning and serve immediately.

Also try

- Play around with different green vegetables: broccoli, courgettes etc.

- Add a few peeled tiger prawns 2 minutes before the end of the cooking time.

Smoked haddock chowder

Delicious one-pot dining, and a great way of getting children to eat some fish and vegetables.

Serves 4-6

4 rashers rindless smoked streaky
   bacon, cut into thin strips
25g (1oz) unsalted butter
1 onion, finely diced
1 tsp soft thyme leaves
1 red pepper, seeded and cut into
   5mm (¼ inch) dice
1 carrot, finely diced
4 medium potatoes, peeled and
   cut into 1cm (½ inch) dice
½ tsp dried chilli flakes (optional)
1 tbsp plain flour
450ml (16fl oz) semi-skimmed
   milk
300ml (10fl oz) double cream
450ml (16fl oz) fish or chicken
   stock
450g (1lb) undyed smoked
   haddock fillet, skinned and cut
   in 2.5cm (1 inch) pieces
115g (4oz) frozen peas
1 x small can sweetcorn, rinsed
   and drained
salt and ground white pepper

1 Cook the bacon in the butter in a large saucepan for 5 minutes, until it has released some of its fat and is starting to crisp.

2 Add the onion, thyme, pepper, carrot, potatoes and chilli, and cook for 8 minutes, until the potatoes start to stick to the bottom of the pan. Add the flour and stir to combine, then cook over a very low heat for 3-4 minutes, stirring continuously.

3 Add some milk and cream a little at a time, stirring, until the flour becomes a paste. Add the remaining milk and cream and the stock, bring to the boil, stirring, reduce the heat and simmer for 12 minutes.

4 Add the haddock, peas and sweetcorn and cook for a further 6 minutes.

5 Season to taste and serve hot with warm crusty bread.

Also try

- Use unsmoked haddock, cod or another white fish instead of smoked haddock; the cooking time stays the same.

- Change the vegetables – some spinach, small broccoli florets or cauliflower go nicely.

- Adults may prefer to replace some of the stock with dry white wine.

A different vegetable soup

This is a way to spice up a good nutritious soup. There's loads of flavour and something a little different, a challenge for the children's taste buds.

Serves 4

25g (1oz) unsalted butter
1 red onion, chopped
2 garlic cloves, finely chopped
175g (6oz) each of turnip, sweet
   potato and pumpkin, peeled and
   cut into 1cm (½ inch) cubes
1 tsp ground coriander
1 tsp ground ginger
1 tbsp chopped spring onions
salt and ground black pepper
1 litre (1¾ pints) vegetable stock
2 tbsp flaked almonds, toasted
1 fresh chilli, seeded and
   chopped
1 tsp caster sugar
25g (1oz) creamed coconut
chopped coriander to garnish

1   Melt the butter in a large non-stick saucepan. Fry the onion and garlic for 6-8 minutes over a medium heat. Add the diced vegetables and fry for 3-4 minutes.

2   Add the ground coriander, ground ginger, spring onions and some salt and pepper. Fry over a low heat for about 5 minutes, stirring frequently.

3   Add the vegetable stock, flaked almonds, chopped chilli and sugar and stir well to mix, then cover and simmer gently for 10-15 minutes, until the vegetables are just tender.

4   Grate the creamed coconut into the soup and stir to mix. Sprinkle with chopped coriander.

5   Ladle into warmed bowls and serve with crusty bread.

Also try

● Add a little smoked bacon to fry with the onion.

● Add some diced green vegetables 2 minutes before the end of the cooking time.

Clean and green chicken salad

I use the Chinese method of poaching chicken, which keeps the meat really juicy and tender. If you are in a hurry, just use a dressing of 4 parts olive oil to 1 part lemon juice or white wine vinegar.

Serves 6

1 small bunch coriander
5 slices fresh root ginger, peeled
1 head garlic, halved horizontally
2 hot dried chillies
1 onion, roughly chopped
1 x 1.6kg (3½lb) free-range
  chicken
1 tsp salt

Salad
125g (4½oz) broccoli florets
85g (3oz) fresh or frozen peas
125g (4½oz) asparagus tips
85g (3oz) sugar-snap peas
2 Little Gem lettuces
2 handfuls baby spinach leaves
2 handfuls rocket leaves
1 bunch spring onions, tops
  removed and thinly sliced

Peanut soy dressing
85g (3oz) smooth peanut butter
2 tbsp sweet soy sauce
1 tbsp runny honey
½ tsp garlic purée
1 tsp chilli oil
2 tbsp rice vinegar

1   Place the coriander, ginger, garlic, chillies, onion and chicken in a pan just large enough to hug the chicken. Top up with cold water to cover the chicken, add the salt and cover with a lid. Bring to the boil, then reduce the heat until the water is just moving on the surface. Simmer gently for 30 minutes, then turn off the heat and allow the chicken to cool in its poaching liquor – ideally overnight in the refrigerator. Check it is cooked through.

2   Meanwhile, make the salad. Have ready a large pan of boiling salted water. Blanch the broccoli florets for 3 minutes, then drain and refresh in cold water. Do the same with the peas and asparagus tips, but for 2 minutes only. Blanch the sugar-snaps for 1 minute only, then drain and refresh in cold water.

3   To make the dressing, blend the peanut butter, soy sauce, honey, garlic, chilli oil and vinegar until smooth. Use water to thin down to a dressing consistency.

4   Remove the chicken from the pan and take off the meat, discarding the skin. Either cut the meat into chunks or finely shred. Coat the meat lightly with some of the dressing. Set aside. Retain the stock as a base for an excellent soup.

5   Separate the lettuce leaves and arrange them with the spinach, rocket and onions over the base of a large platter. Toss the blanched vegetables with the remaining dressing and arrange over the leaves. Scatter chicken over the vegetables.

Also try

- Use cooked loin of pork instead of the poached chicken.

- For a more adult taste, combine a handful of coriander leaves and 14 shredded mint leaves with the vegetables.

Tuna and bean salad

A classic Italian appetizer that appeals to most tastes.

Serves 2-4

1 x 400g can cannellini beans, drained, rinsed and drained

½ red onion, finely sliced

1 tbsp roughly chopped flat-leaf parsley

4 tbsp extra virgin olive oil

1 tbsp freshly squeezed lemon juice

salt and ground black pepper

1 x 200g can tuna in olive oil, drained and flaked

1 In a bowl, mix together the beans, onion and parsley.

2 Combine the olive oil with the lemon juice, salt and black pepper and pour over the mix.

3 Add the tuna and toss to combine. Serve immediately.

Also try

- Any type of canned beans works with this dish.

- Mash the beans and place them on a crostini or in a wrap, then top with the tuna.

Smoked mackerel and warm potato salad

Everyone benefits from eating two portions of fish a week, one of which should be an oily fish, and this recipe fits the bill. Most children find this an enjoyable way of eating fish, and it's a great salad for adults as well.

Serves 4

450g (1lb) waxy new potatoes, washed
salt
3 hard-boiled free-range eggs, roughly chopped
4 spring onions, finely sliced
4 fillets smoked mackerel, skinned and flaked
2 lemons, halved

Dressing
1 tsp Dijon mustard
3 tbsp white wine or cider vinegar
1 tsp runny honey
1/4 tsp salt
a good few twists of ground black pepper
9 tbsp extra virgin olive oil
2 shallots, finely chopped
1 tbsp snipped chives
1 dill-flavoured gherkin, finely chopped

1 For the dressing, combine the mustard, vinegar and honey and whisk. Add the salt and pepper, then drizzle on the olive oil while still whisking. Add the remaining ingredients and leave for the flavours to infuse for 15 minutes. Whisk before using.

2 Meanwhile, place the new potatoes in a saucepan, cover with cold salted water, bring to the boil and simmer for 15-20 minutes, depending on size, or until tender. Drain and, when cool enough to handle, cut into 1cm (½ inch) slices.

3 Place the warm potato slices in a bowl with the hard-boiled eggs and spring onions, and add enough dressing to coat.

4 Place a layer of the potato mix on the bottom of a platter, and scatter over some flaked mackerel. Top with another layer of potatoes, then mackerel, and so on. Drizzle each layer of mackerel with dressing. Serve immediately with lemon halves to squeeze over.

Also try

- Use medium-rare cold roast beef or cooked prawns instead of the mackerel.

- Some children prefer mayonnaise to vinaigrette dressing. Fold a little horseradish into the mayonnaise if you want a more sophisticated flavour.

Lunchboxes

If I had my way, I would ban the idea of lunchboxes at school. The problem is peer pressure. You can be the most diligent, caring parent in the world, but it's all to no avail if your little darling spots the alternative lunchbox – the one their friend is eating; the one with crisps, a chocolate bar, a fizzy drink and an over-sugary yoghurt. Peer pressure makes it very difficut to persuade your child to take a healthy lunchbox to school and, even if he does, it's impossible to guarantee that he will actually eat it rather than throw it into the school bin.

It is very hard for parents to resist 'pester power' – the constant badgering of a child who has been brainwashed by television adverts, magazines and posters – so in the end it is no surprise when the parent just gives up and goes with the flow. The trick, I find, is to compromise, for the occasional bag of crisps is not going to be deadly. Come to an arrangement with your children that, say, mondays, wednesdays and fridays are good food days, and tuesdays and thursdays mean just one little treat from the supermarket magnet.

In my view, the way to be seen as the coolest parent on the planet is to prepare home-made treats that make your offspring's lunchbox *the* most talked about in the playground – the lunchbox that makes all the others untempting. It's all about balance; the right balance nutritionally and in terms of variety both on the day and over the week.

The truth is that when temptation or choice is put in front of a child, quite naturally he will make the wrong choice: he will choose something he knows he likes, and for most children that is usually the unhealthy kid's option. So it's back to the theme of the book: to regain control of your kids you must lay down the rules, tell the children their parameters, and dictate to them their diet. The old-fashioned phrase, 'Mum knows best', should have stood the test of time, but unfortunately it hasn't. Parents must lead the way and schools need to follow the same guidelines.

'The phrase "mum knows best" should have stood the test of time.'

A pasta salad with Oriental undertones

Children love a hint of sweetness, which you mustn't see as a problem, as it can be harnessed as a way of getting them to eat healthy food, as with this honey and sweet chilli dressing.

Serves 2

200g (7oz) fresh fettuccine or egg noodles
salt
1 tsp sesame oil
1 tbsp vegetable oil
25g (1oz) grated or julienned carrot
25g (1oz) raw mini cauliflower florets
25g (1oz) peeled, seeded and diced cucumber
½ red pepper, seeded and diced
2 spring onions, finely sliced
55g (2oz) baby sweetcorn, finely sliced
2 tbsp runny honey
2 tsp sweet chilli sauce
juice of 1 lime or ½ lemon
25g (1oz) shelled peanuts, chopped (optional)

1 Cook the pasta in plenty of salted boiling water according to the pack's instructions, until al dente. Drain and rinse under cold water, then drain again and toss with the oils to stop it sticking together.

2 Combine all the vegetables, then fold them into the pasta.

3 Combine the honey, chilli sauce and citrus juice for a dressing, stirring until blended. Pour this over the salad and toss to combine.

4 Divide between the lunchboxes and sprinkle with peanuts for added crunch if you like.

Also try

- Most vegetables will work, including tomatoes.

- Add diced cooked chicken or ham or diced Cheddar or Feta.

- If your child has a peanut allergy, you'll almost certainly know about it. Leave the peanuts and sesame oil out if necessary. It's worth checking if your child's school has a non-peanut policy before including peanuts.

Chicken, sweetcorn and pasta salad

A favourite every time, providing the right mix of protein and carbohydrates. I prefer the children to eat a light dressing rather than mayo, but that's up to you.

Serves 2

115g (4oz) farfalle or penne,
1 cooked free-range chicken
  breast or smoked chicken
  breast, cut into bite-sized
  pieces
55g (2oz) canned or frozen
  sweetcorn
4 dried apricots, finely diced
2 spring onions, finely sliced
85g (3oz) white cabbage, finely
  diced
25g (1oz) sultanas or raisins
2 rashers cooked crispy bacon,
  crumbled

Dressing
2 tbsp good olive oil
2 tsp cider vinegar or white wine
  vinegar
1 tsp Dijon mustard
1 tsp runny honey
salt and ground black pepper

1 Cook the pasta in plenty of salted boiling water according to the pack instructions, until al dente. Drain and rinse under cold water, then drain again and leave to cool.

2 Combine the pasta with the remaining salad ingredients except for the crispy bacon.

3 Whisk together the dressing ingredients and season to taste.

4 Toss the salad with the dressing. Divide between the two lunchboxes and scatter with the crispy bacon.

Also try

- Substitute canned tuna for the chicken.

- Add some batons of carrot, tiny florets of raw cauliflower, or diced radish or cucumber for extra crunch.

- Use chopped peanuts instead of crispy bacon for the topping.

- Use shredded Little Gem lettuce instead of cabbage and eat the salad immediately.

Poached chicken club sandwich with avocado, roast tomato and salad

Club sandwiches are great at any time of day or night. Some children may find the taste of the avocados not to their liking, in which case omit them.

Serves 2

2 half baguettes (mini French sticks)

2 tbsp mayonnaise

2 tbsp tomato chutney or salsa

6 thin slices Italian salami

1 small Little Gem lettuce, separated into leaves

8 roast tomato halves

½ avocado, peeled, stoned and sliced

6 thin slices cooked ham

175g (6oz) poached free-range chicken, thinly sliced (see page 40)

salt and ground black pepper

1 Cut the baguettes lengthways, halfway through. Spread the bottom half with mayonnaise and the top side with tomato chutney or salsa.

2 On the bottom half, arrange the salami, then the lettuce, then the tomatoes, avocado, ham and chicken, then season to taste. Press the top half of the baguette downwards.

3 Wrap in greaseproof paper or clingfilm.

Also try

- Sometimes you may not have time to cook the tomatoes, in which case substitute with sun-blushed or sun-dried.

- Adults may prefer a smearing of olive tapenade instead of the tomato pickle.

- Thinly sliced crisp apple or pear makes a good substitute for tomato or avocado, but only if you're going to eat the sandwich immediately.

Lifestyle and carbohydrates

Whether you're planning a lunchbox or a lunch at home, on the nutritional front you will need to assess your child before the meal. Is he/she wildly active, or a bit of a couch slouch? You need to choose foods to match the requirements of each child – and you, as parent, know best.

Carbohydrates are the principal fuel or energy source for the body, and they come in two forms: fast-releasing and slow-releasing. Fast-releasing carbohydrate foods include sugar, honey, malt, sweet and most refined foods; slow-releasing carbohydrate foods include whole grains, vegetables and fresh fruit. In what is now known as the Glycaemic Index or GI, carbohydrate foods are ranked based on the rate at which they raise blood glucose levels. High-GI foods – the high-releasing ones – break down quickly, raising blood glucose quickly. In children this can cause a 'high' feeling, followed by a fairly quick descent, by lack of energy and concentration, a swift return of hunger, and mood change. Low-GI foods – the slow releasing ones – break down more slowly, and children will remain on a more even keel for longer.

If your child is full of energy, he/she will be burning off calories, so potential 'fat' issues are not the primary worry. What you need to offer – and not just for lunch – are medium- or low-GI foods such as pasta, fresh fruit, sandwiches made with whole-grain bread, wraps, natural yoghurts, unrefined whole-grain cereals etc. Energy-giving carbs do not need to mean sugar (although, after a busy and active morning at school or at play, your energetic child may benefit from a high-GI drink of squash, a piece of melon or a handful of raisins or other dried fruit to stoke the boiler again). For, ironic as it may seem, some foods that we think of as 'bad' are actually quite low-GI, and the opposite is true as well: 'bad' chocolate, for instance, is low-GI, while 'good' melon is high-GI!

On the other hand, if your child is a bit of a sofa loafer, with a tendency to sit for hours in front of a computer or Game Boy, then you have to think about how you can safely reduce their calorie intake, but still maintain enough energy for concentration levels.

Another irony of GI is that many fat and protein foods are rated as medium- or low-GI because both fat and protein slow down the absorption of carbohydrate (thus the categorization of chocolate above). What you will need to concentrate on are low-fat, medium-to-low-GI foods: grilled lean meat (preferably poultry, without skin), pulses, and plenty of lightly cooked vegetables and fresh salads. You will have to avoid crisps, biscuits and sweet energy bars. Something like a baked potato would be a good lunch, as it is full of fibre; as it is high-GI, top it with some low-GI baked beans, which immediately turn the meal into a medium-GI meal – and don't involve too many calories. Try, also, to get your couch slouch to be a bit more mobile, and take at least a little exercise every day, which will help to burn off some calories.

'Carbohydrates are the principal energy source.'

Asian wrap

Introduce this wrap to your children and they may not even notice they are only eating fruit and veg.

Serves 2

85g (3oz) thin rice noodles

75ml (2½fl oz) rice wine vinegar

finely grated zest and juice of 1
  unwaxed lime

1 tbsp *nam pla* (fish sauce)

a pinch of crushed red chilli
  flakes (optional)

1 carrot, grated

¼ cucumber, peeled, seeded and
  diced

½ mango, peeled, stoned and
  chopped

4 spring onions, finely sliced

1 tbsp chopped coriander

1 tbsp chopped mint

½ tbsp sesame seeds

1 Little Gem lettuce, shredded

2 x 22-25cm (9-10 inch) soft flour
  tortillas

1   Cover the noodles with hot water in a large bowl, and leave to sit for 10 minutes. Drain completely; it is important to remove all excess water.

2   Combine the vinegar, lime juice and zest, fish sauce and chilli flakes in a large bowl. Add the well-drained noodles and toss to coat evenly. Add the carrot, cucumber, mango, spring onions, herbs and sesame seeds and mix well.

3   Place some lettuce on each tortilla.

4   Divide the noodle mixture among the lettuce leaf-lined tortillas and roll up, tucking in the ends.

Also try

● A couple of shredded radishes add extra crunch.

● Use chopped peanuts instead of sesame seeds.

● Use chopped fresh pineapple instead of mango.

● A little shredded cooked chicken or ham can be added.

Thai wrap

Time to introduce the children to the definitive flavours of Thailand. Not a wrap for when you are in a rush, this one takes a little time to prepare.

Serves 2

125ml (4fl oz) coconut milk

1 stalk lemongrass

½ tbsp Thai red curry paste

1 garlic clove, crushed to a paste with salt

1 tbsp soft brown sugar

salt

225g (8oz) boneless, skinless chicken breasts, cut into thin strips

1 tbsp fresh lime juice

1 tbsp olive oil

1 courgette, diced

1 pak-choi, finely shredded

½ red onion, finely chopped

115g (4oz) freshly cooked jasmine rice, warm

1 tbsp chopped basil

1 tsp chopped mint

2 x 22-25cm (9-10 inch) soft flour tortillas

1 Combine the coconut milk, lemongrass, curry paste, garlic, brown sugar and ½ tsp salt in a medium saucepan over a medium heat. Bring to a simmer and cook until the liquid thickens, about 6-8 minutes.

2 Add the chicken and cook for 5 minutes, until cooked, then remove from the heat. Add the lime juice and set aside.

3 Heat the olive oil in a large non-stick pan over a medium heat. Add the courgette, pak-choi and onion, season with salt, and cook until the vegetables are tender, about 5-7 minutes. Transfer to a large bowl.

4 Add the vegetables and rice to the chicken in coconut sauce, and mix well. Allow to cool. Fold in the herbs.

5 Drain any excess sauce from the mixture. Divide between the tortillas, then roll up, tucking in the ends.

Also try

- Try some different vegetables: spring onions, roast pumpkin, roast peppers.

Spanish tortilla with spinach, goat's cheese and ricotta

I love tortilla (Spanish omelette), and while the Spanish people might not approve, it proves a great vehicle for all sorts of additions and flavours.

Serves 6

450ml (16fl oz) olive oil

5 medium potatoes, peeled and
   cut into 5mm (¼ inch) slices

2 large onions, thinly sliced

2 garlic cloves, crushed

2 tbsp finely chopped parsley

1 tsp finely chopped thyme

coarse salt and ground black
   pepper

a pinch of paprika

225g (8oz) goat's cheese,
   crumbled

175g (6oz) cooked spinach,
   squeezed dry and chopped

8 free-range eggs, beaten with
   4 tbsp double cream

115g (4oz) ricotta cheese, drained

1   Preheat the oven to 170°C/325°F/gas mark 3. Heat the oil in a deep frying pan. Add the potatoes, alternating in layers with the onions. Cook gently, covered, until the potatoes are just tender, about 15 minutes (they should remain separate, but should not brown). Tip the potatoes and onions into a colander, saving the oil. Put the potato mix in a bowl.

2   In a frying pan, heat a little of the reserved oil (use the rest for a great flavoured dressing). Add the garlic, parsley, thyme, salt, pepper, paprika, and finally the goat's cheese, and cook for 3 minutes. Mix with the spinach, potatoes and onions and season to taste.

3   Transfer this mixture to a large, shallow non-stick frying pan that will go in the oven. The dish may be made in advance to this point.

4   Pour the eggs and cream over the potatoes, then dot with ricotta, shake and place briefly over a low heat to set the bottom, then place in the oven for 15-20 minutes, or until the eggs have set. Allow to cool.

5   Turn out on to a plate. Serve with a large mixed salad.

Also try

Try different flavours, always using the potatoes as a base:

- Onion, cooked bacon and grated Cheddar; broccoli and blue cheese; or sweated leeks, cooked bacon and Gorgonzola.

- Something fishy, such as flaked cooked salmon and dill.

- Red pepper, olive and sun-dried tomato.

My Scotch eggs

Some of the shop-bought Scotch eggs are very dull, and the eggs pale, so this recipe is well worth the effort.

Serves 4

½ onion, very finely chopped
1 tsp finely chopped sage
½ tsp soft thyme leaves
1 tsp Worcestershire sauce
1 tsp Dijon mustard
½ tsp salt
¼ tsp ground black pepper
1 tbsp chopped parsley
5 very fresh free-range eggs, 1 of
  which is beaten
225g (8oz) sausage meat
plain flour for dusting
6 tbsp natural dried breadcrumbs
  (no orange ones please)
vegetable oil for deep-frying

1   In a frying pan, cook the onion, sage and thyme in a little oil over a low heat for 15 minutes, until the onions are soft but without colour. Add the Worcestershire sauce and mustard and stir. Allow to cool, then mix in the salt, pepper and parsley.

2   Meanwhile, place 4 eggs carefully in boiling water and cook for 7 minutes. Immediately plunge them in cold water and leave for 5 minutes before shelling carefully. Combine the onion mix with the sausagemeat and knead well.

3   Flour the shelled eggs. Divide the sausagemeat into 4 pieces and flatten each piece until it is an even thickness, 10cm (4 inches) in diameter. Mould each piece of meat around an egg, making sure it is evenly coated.

4   Dust the meat with a fine coating of flour, then roll in the beaten egg. Roll the eggs in breadcrumbs. Set aside.

5   Heat the oil in a deep-fat fryer until it reaches 180°C/350°F or until it browns a piece of bread in about 30 seconds. Cook the eggs in the oil for 6-8 minutes, turning once, until golden brown and crisp. Drain on kitchen paper and cool at room temperature, then refrigerate in an airtight container.

Also try

- Change the herbs to parsley and lemon zest or oregano and garlic, adding everything where the parsley is normally added except the garlic, which should be added with the onion.

- Omit the Worcestershire sauce and mustard.

- Mix some grated Parmesan into the breadcrumbs.

- Coat the eggs in finely chopped peanuts before cooking.

- Make mini eggs for a party using quails' eggs.

Fruity lunch bars

These are an alternative to the normal cereal bars that are available from the shops. They are an instant energy-giving snack or can be offered as an alternative to a pud. Most children will probably eat these well in advance of lunch.

Makes 12

2 tbsp runny honey

115g (4oz) unsalted butter

25g (1oz) dark muscovado sugar

55g (2oz) rolled oats

55g (2oz) bran flakes, lightly crushed

25g (1oz) dried cherries

25g (1oz) dried blueberries

25g (1oz) dried organic apricots, chopped

25g (1oz) sunflower seeds

2 tbsp sesame seeds

1   Preheat the oven to 180°C/350°F/gas mark 4. Lightly butter and flour an 18-20cm (7-8 inch) square, shallow cake tin.

2   Heat the honey, butter and sugar in a saucepan and cook until the sugar has dissolved and it has all come together in a smooth emulsion.

3   Fold in the remaining ingredients and stir well to combine, then press the mixture into the prepared cake tin, smoothing the surface.

4   Bake in the preheated oven for 25-30 minutes, until golden brown. Remove from the oven and allow to cool for 10 minutes before marking the surface with indentations to make 12 bars.

5   Transfer to a wire cooling rack, allow to cool, then cut in 12 bars. Store in an airtight container. Wrap each bar in greaseproof paper before adding to the children's lunchboxes.

Also try

- You can play with different dried fruits or nuts and seeds, so long as you stick to the same weight ratio between the toffee mix, the oats and bran, and the fruits and nuts. The fruit could be as simple as mixed peel or sultanas and raisins, or chopped dried mango, pineapple or apple would make a nice change.

- If you have no bran flakes, used all rolled oats instead.

Quick onion and mint breadsticks

A pleasant little snack, perfect with a dip or just a quick nibble.

Makes about 32

450g (1lb) plain flour
2 tbsp baking powder
1 tsp salt
225ml (8fl oz) boiling water
2 tsp runny honey
a small pinch of chilli flakes
2 tbsp chopped mint
3 spring onions, finely chopped
2 tbsp cooked chopped shallots
1 tsp ground black pepper
extra virgin olive oil

1   In a food processor, combine the flour, baking powder and salt. Combine the boiling water with the honey and pour this mixture slowly through the feed tube of the processor with the machine running until a ball of dough forms. You may need more or less water depending on the type of flour you use.

2   Flour a work surface and tip the dough on to the flour. Knead the dough with the heel of your hand for 3-4 minutes until pliable. Wrap the dough in clingfilm and leave to rest for 30 minutes in the refrigerator.

3   Divide the dough into 8 portions, then roll out into rectangles about 1cm (½ inch) thick. Sprinkle each with some of the chilli flakes, mint, spring onions, cooked shallots and pepper. Fold in half, then roll out again to the same thickness. Cut each rectangle into 4 fingers. Allow to rest for 30 minutes.

4   Brush a large frying pan with a little olive oil. Brush each onion breadstick with olive oil. Cook the bread in batches for 3-4 minutes on each side until golden brown.

5   When the breadsticks are cooked, drain on kitchen paper and keep warm in the oven or cool and store in an airtight container.

Also try

● Sprinkle rock salt on the breadsticks once you have cooked them.

● Use different herbs or spices instead of onions.

Fruit spice slices

We've already established that there are times when children need lunchbox-treats – not everyday but once or twice a week. These are perfect.

Serves 12-16

1 tsp bicarbonate of soda

4 tbsp semi-skimmed milk

115g (4oz) unsalted butter, softened

115g (4oz) dark muscovado sugar

2 free-range eggs, beaten

225g (8oz) plain or cake flour

3 tbsp black treacle

3 tbsp golden syrup

1 tsp ground cinnamon

½ tsp ground ginger

2 tbsp dried cherries

2 tbsp chopped dried apricots

1 Preheat the oven to 180°C/350°F/gas mark 4. Line the bottom of a greased cake tin, ideally rectangular (30 x 20 x 5cm/12 x 8 x 2 inches) with parchment or oiled greaseproof paper.

2 Whisk the bicarbonate of soda into the milk.

3 In a large mixing bowl, beat together the butter and sugar with an electric hand-whisk until light and fluffy. Add the eggs a little at a time, alternating with a little flour, and beat until well mixed.

4 Add the treacle and syrup, then sift in the remaining flour with the cinnamon and ginger. Add the milk, then beat everything together. Finally fold in the dried fruit.

5 Spoon the mixture into the prepared tin, smoothing the top with a spatula. Place the tin in the centre of the preheated oven and cook for about 1 hour, or until a skewer inserted into the centre comes out clean.

6 Allow to cool in the tin, then turn out and cut into 12-16 slices. Store in an airtight container.

Also try

- A few nibbed almonds add a nice crunch.

- A soft cheese frosting could be spread on top when the slices have cooled.

Fresh lemonade

I make this lemonade base up ahead of time and dilute it when required. A drink of fresh lemonade is better every time than some fizzy number from a vending machine or a can. The citric acid and tartaric acid are available from larger chemists.

Makes 2 litres (3½ pints)

1 litre (1¾ pints) water
1.5 kg (3lb 5oz) golden caster sugar
juice and finely grated zest of 9 unwaxed lemons
25g (1oz) citric acid
25g (1oz) tartaric acid

1 Combine all the ingredients in a saucepan and simmer gently until the sugar dissolves, then cook for a further 5 minutes.

2 Allow to cool, strain and bottle in washed-out mineral water bottles.

3 Dilute with still or fizzy mineral water when required, according to taste.

Luxury fruit salad

I don't know about you, but I find it easier to get my children to eat the more exotic fruits than the usual apples and oranges.

Serves 4

1 mango
1 papaya
115g (4oz) watermelon
½ sweet melon
½ pineapple
85g (3oz) shredded fresh coconut
2 passion fruits, pulp and seeds only
juice and finely grated zest of 2 unwaxed limes
2 tbsp caster sugar
150ml (5fl oz) orange juice
2 tsp chopped mint (optional)

1 Peel and stone the mango, peel and seed the papaya, watermelon and sweet melon, and peel and core the pineapple. Cut all these fruits into bite-sized pieces.

2 Mix all the ingredients together, and chill in the refrigerator until ready to serve.

After-school dinners

After-school suppers were always looked forward to when I was a child, even when I was at boarding school. Although the food was the pits at school, the principle remained the same: it was a time for gathering around a table with mates and enjoying a good gossip; enjoying conversation.

It should be the same at home – enjoying a meal with the family, having the occasional school-friend over and discussing your day, sorting out the world in miniature. Sadly, too often this is not the case, with many families falling back on ready-meals or takeaways, which are often eaten in front of the telly, where conversation is non-existent. It's sad, because if you study families in other countries, where they take meal times seriously, you will notice a bond is created that lasts into adulthood; a bond that ensures families look after each other in later life, keeping them together.

It's often not easy – especially if both parents work and don't come home until late. Sometimes we all feel too exhausted to cook the kids something decent or even play a game with them. But this tiredness can often be reduced by diet. Eating the wrong sort of carbs can play havoc with our blood sugar levels, making us constantly need to snack. If we pick at sugary foods we get a surge in energy that will be followed by a crash. This vicious spiral has a terrible effect on our energy levels, meaning that once we are home we haven't the enthusiasm to cook for our family.

After-school suppers don't need to be difficult if we're organised. Keep the dishes simple and nutritious, don't make it hard for yourself, and make some things ahead. And you need a rule: you mustn't wimp out to the badgering of your children wanting to watch television. Meal times are meal times and everyone should attend. When the children are young, make meals fun: introduce variety with new flavours to get them feeling that food is part of life, not just something that keeps them alive. The key to your children not becoming fussy is to eat with them, eating the same food.

'Keep dishes simple
and nutritious and make
some things ahead.'

Creamy scrambled eggs in roast mushroom cups

Most scrambled eggs are curdy and very eggy, which sounds obvious I know, but once in a while it makes a change to have a more French style of whipped eggs.

Serves 4

8 large cup mushrooms, white skin peeled, stalks removed
½ tsp finely chopped soft thyme leaves
salt and ground black pepper
2 tbsp olive oil
6 free-range eggs
45ml (1½fl oz) double cream
1 tsp creamed horseradish
25g (1oz) unsalted butter
soft thyme leaves to garnish

1   Preheat the oven to 180°C/350°F/gas mark 4.

2   Place the mushrooms in a bowl, and sprinkle with the thyme, ¼ tsp each of salt and pepper, and olive oil. Toss gently to combine without breaking the mushrooms.

3   Arrange the mushrooms, black face up, on a rack over a baking tray, place in the preheated oven and cook for 15-20 minutes, basting from time to time with their juices.

4   Meanwhile, whisk together the eggs, cream, horseradish and seasoning to taste.

5   Heat the butter in a non-stick frying pan or saucepan until foaming. Add the egg mixture and whisk continuously until cooked. The eggs should be cooked over a medium to low heat until set but still very soft; this should take no longer than 3-4 minutes. Remove the eggs from the heat when quite soft as they will continue to cook.

6   Remove the mushrooms from the oven, and spoon some of the scrambled eggs into each one. Serve on or with buttered multi-grain toast with thyme leaves sprinkled over.

Also try

- Substitute tomatoes for mushrooms.

- Add snipped chives and tarragon to the egg mix before cooking.

- Some kids prefer their scrambled eggs more chunky. To achieve this, do not whisk the egg and cream mixture – simply pour it into the pan and stir while cooking.

Welsh rarebit with tomatoes and spinach

This dish is all about camouflage: wilted spinach combined with a cheesy mixture to make a bubbly rarebit. It makes a light supper packed full of goodness. The Welsh rarebit mix can be made well ahead and is always a useful standby.

Serves 4

55g (2oz) unsalted butter

2 tsp English or Dijon mustard

1 tsp Worcestershire sauce

½ tsp Tabasco sauce

4 tbsp bitter, stout or Guinness (optional), or apple or tomato juice

250g (9oz) Cheddar or Lancashire cheese, grated

4 free-range egg yolks

1 x 125g bag baby spinach, washed

2 tbsp olive oil

salt and ground black pepper

4 thick slices country bread

175g (6oz) sun-dried tomatoes, finely chopped

1   Gently heat the butter, mustard, Worcestershire sauce, Tabasco and beer together, whisking all the time, until simmering. Immediately add the cheese and stir while it melts. Do not allow to boil. Remove from the heat and set aside to cool.

2   When it is at room temperature, beat in the yolks. This mix can be stored for 2 weeks in the refrigerator, depending on the freshness of the eggs. Bring to room temperature to use.

3   Meanwhile, in a large saucepan cook the spinach in the olive oil with a pinch of salt and pepper until wilted. Allow to cool, then squeeze out most of the liquid.

4   Put the spinach in a food processor with half the egg mix and blend until smooth. Keep the remaining mix for another use.

5   Toast the bread on both sides, then spread with the spinach rarebit. Dot the surface with the sun-dried tomatoes, then place under a hot grill until the cheese mixture is bubbling.

Also try

- Try a topping of cooked bacon instead of the sun-dried tomatoes.

- Spread the rarebit mixture over cooked broccoli or cauliflower and pop under the grill.

- Many children love olives, so you could spread the toast with an olive tapenade before topping with the rarebit. Alternatively a sun-dried tomato or red pepper paste is good.

- Top with a poached or fried egg.

Pumpkin gnocchi with sage

A dish I learnt from Gennaro Contaldo, Jamie Oliver's mate and father figure; a lovely guy with great cooking ability and a good sense of fun.

Serves 6

1.7kg (3¾lb) pumpkin, peeled, seeded and cut into wedges
extra virgin olive oil for drizzling
1 tbsp finely chopped sage
2-3 garlic cloves
600ml (1 pint) vegetable stock
plain flour, as required
rice flour
salt and ground black pepper
4 tbsp freshly grated Parmesan

Sauce
3 tbsp olive oil
1 tbsp finely chopped sage

1　Preheat the oven to 190°C/375°F/gas mark 5. Cut 200g (7oz) of the pumpkin flesh into 5mm (¼ inch) pieces. Set aside. Roast the remaining pumpkin wedges with a little olive oil, the sage and garlic in the preheated oven for 45 minutes, or until soft and caramelized, turning at times.

2　Place the roasted pumpkin in a blender and whiz to a creamy consistency. Alternatively, mash with a fork. Remove 225g (8oz) of this and set aside for the sauce.

3　Put the rest of the mashed pumpkin and the stock in a saucepan and bring to the boil. Reduce the heat and stir in the flour. It is ready when the mixture comes away from the sides of the pan. Remove from the heat and allow to cool.

4　Place the cooled mixture on a clean rice-floured surface and, with the help of some more rice flour, roll large pieces of the dough into sausage shapes, then slice into 2cm (¾ inch) pieces. Bring a large saucepan of salted water to the boil.

5　Meanwhile, to make the sauce, heat the olive oil in a frying pan and fry the sage until brown. Add the raw pumpkin cubes and pan-fry for 2 minutes, until cooked. Then add the reserved roasted pumpkin purée. Sieve and keep warm.

6　Drop the gnocchi into boiling water and simmer until they rise to the top. Lift them out with a slotted spoon, drain well and add to the sauce. Serve on individual plates, with a sprinkle of Parmesan and a drizzle of extra virgin olive oil.

Also try

● Substitute rosemary for sage, chopping it well.

Good fats and bad fats

When it comes to food, we don't know whether we're coming or going. Few weeks pass without a media food scare. We're told one thing only to discover a couple of years later that the scientists got it wrong. Think of cholesterol in eggs, shellfish and offal; we were advised not to eat those foods on a regular basis only to discover our own livers are capable of dealing with dietary cholesterol.

On the other hand, saturated fats – fats from animals, including dairy fats – can affect your cholesterol levels, although probably not to the extent some people would have us believe. Most of our cholesterol levels are genetic and, without the use of drugs (statins), will not change much through diet. Having said that, fats are heavy in calories, so over-consumption will have an effect on your weight.

I love the flavour of most fats. Most meats in our supermarkets come from animals reared to be lean. This results in meat with no fatty marbling and very little outer coating of fat, which can make it dry and tasteless. Our pork is a shadow of its former self, our beef is bright red and bland, our ducks are skinny. We can make our animals fat-free, but our eating habits have had the opposite effect on our bodies. Over 50 per cent of adults are fat or obese and there has been a big growth in childhood obesity.

We concentrate too much on criticising saturated fats and not enough on education. I always advise cooking with the fat intact, then removing it afterwards. If you want to reduce your saturated fat intake, remove the roast chicken skin after cooking; remove the fat from the steak before you eat it; when making a stew, cook it the day before, allow it to cool, refrigerate and remove the solidified fat from the surface before reheating. Cook with olive oil instead of butter, although I'd prefer you to use butter on bread, spread thinly, rather than some of the low-fat spreads, as these can contain all sorts of nasties, including hydrogenated vegetable oil, which has been proven to raise cholesterol levels.

Common sense must be the deciding factor. Undoubtedly some saturated fats are good for you if eaten in sensible proportions. They're good for the brain and other parts of the body. We need them but, like everything else, we can overdo it. I've had parents ask me whether they should stop milk, butter and cheese being served to their children. My answer would be no, as long as they're part of a balanced diet. All these fats contain important amounts of calcium and other nutrients essential for bone and growth development; it could be dangerous to lose them from your child's diet.

The fats you need to be aware of are hidden fats found in some foods: cereals, ready-meals and pre-prepared sandwiches, and snack foods. Always read the nutritional information on the label.

'Cook with the fat intact; remove it after cooking'

Curly herby frittata

This is a very different way of serving eggs, which turns them into something a bit like pasta. It's good on its own or as an accompaniment to grilled food.

Serves 4

100g (3½oz) spinach leaves, washed, stalks removed
a handful of rocket leaves, torn
a handful of flat-leaf parsley leaves
8 large free-range eggs
salt and ground black pepper
unsalted butter for frying
2 tbsp fresh double cream
4 tbsp freshly grated Parmesan

1   Boil the spinach, rocket and parsley leaves in 1cm (½ inch) water for 2 minutes. Drain and refresh under cold water. Squeeze dry and place the mix in a food processor. Blend until smooth.

2   Beat the eggs with some salt and pepper, then pour into the food processor with the greens and blend until the mixture is smooth and a uniform green.

3   Brush a non-stick pan with a little melted butter to warm through and set over a medium heat. Pour in a little of the egg mix and swirl in the pan, coating the bottom as you would with a pancake. Cook for about 45 seconds, then turn over and cook for a further 10 seconds. The frittata should be paper-thin.

4   Remove from the pan and repeat until you have used up the mix. Depending on your cooking skills, you should produce 6-8 frittatas. (They can be made ahead and each frittata layered between clingfilm or greaseproof paper. Cut into strips just before reheating.)

5   Roll up the frittatas and cut into 1cm (½ inch) strips that resemble green pasta.

6   Pan-fry the frittata strips in a little butter, stirring very carefully, then add the cream, Parmesan and seasoning and toss to combine.

7   Serve with a tomato salad as a starter or as an accompaniment to a piece of grilled meat or fish.

Also try

● Add some tomato and basil or chilli and garlic to the sauce.

Tomato and basil poached fish

A good, healthy one-pot dish that is fine for lunch or dinner, and a tasty way of encouraging children to eat fish and vegetables.

Serves 4

1 tbsp olive oil
2 onions, sliced
2 garlic cloves, finely chopped
12 new potatoes, diced
125ml (4fl oz) vegetable or fish
  stock
2 x 400g cans chopped tomatoes
salt and ground black pepper
4 x 200g (7oz) firm white fish
  fillets
2 handfuls baby spinach leaves
1 tbsp chopped basil

1   Preheat the oven to 200°C/400°F/gas mark 6.

2   Heat a deep frying pan over a medium heat. Add the oil, onion and garlic and cook for 8 minutes, until the onion is soft. Add the potatoes and stock, cover and cook for 5 minutes. Add the tomatoes and seasoning, and stir to combine. Cook, uncovered, or until the mixture has reduced and thickened slightly, about 10 minutes.

3   Place the fish in a baking dish, top with the tomato mixture and cook in the preheated oven for 12 minutes.

4   To serve, remove the fish from the sauce, and keep warm. Stir the spinach and basil into the sauce, and cook until the spinach has wilted.

5   Spoon the sauce over the fish and serve immediately.

Also try

- Add a little chopped smoked streaky bacon to the onions before cooking.

- Choose monkfish for a more luxurious dish.

Chinese fried rice with peas and prawns

Anything with flavoured rice seems to go down a treat.

Serves 4

4 spring onions, finely sliced

1 tbsp groundnut or vegetable oil

2 tsp grated fresh root ginger,
Lazy Ginger, or ginger purée

½ red pepper, seeded and finely
diced

225g (8oz) raw peeled prawns,
deveined, and cut into
1cm (½ inch) pieces

55g (2oz) smoked streaky bacon,
cut in small lardons

2 free-range eggs, beaten

2 tsp sesame oil

½ tsp salt

¼ tsp ground white pepper

115g (4oz) frozen peas, cooked for
2 minutes

1 tbsp light soy sauce

450g (1lb) freshly cooked rice

1   In a wok, pan-fry the spring onions in the oil for 1 minute
then add the ginger and red pepper and cook for a further
2 minutes over a medium heat.

2   Add the prawns and bacon and cook for a further
2 minutes.

3   Meanwhile, combine the beaten eggs with the sesame oil
and 2 tbsp water. Season with the salt and pepper.

4   Fold the egg into the wok ingredients and, stirring
continuously, cook for 1 minute. Add the peas and soy
sauce, then increase the heat and add the cooked rice. Stir
vigorously to incorporate everything and break the cooked
egg into small pieces.

5   When the rice is piping hot, serve immediately.

Also try

- A splash of Shaoxing rice wine instead of water adds an
adult dimension.

- Try a variety of vegetables: shredded mangetout or cabbage, thinly
sliced carrot, a handful of baby spinach leaves.

Oriental salmon with Asian slaw

My children love Oriental flavours and are now raising the stakes by experimenting more with ingredients such as chilli. These salmon kebabs always go down a treat, although you may have to wean the kids gently on to no-mayo coleslaw.

Serves 4

Salmon

2 garlic cloves, mashed to a paste
  with a little salt

75ml (2½fl oz) *kecap manis*
  (sweet soy sauce)

2 tbsp sesame oil

1 tbsp vegetable oil

550g (1¼lb) salmon fillet, cut into
  2.5cm (1 inch) cubes

Slaw

225g (8oz) Savoy or white
  cabbage, very finely shredded

1 carrot, grated or cut into fine
  shreds

¼ cucumber, peeled, cut in half
  lengthways, seeded and cut
  into 5mm (¼ inch) half-moons

6 radishes, thinly sliced

12 mint leaves, thinly sliced

a small bunch of coriander, leaves
  only

4 tbsp lime juice

1 tbsp runny honey

2 tbsp light soy sauce

1   For the salmon, whisk together the first 4 ingredients, then add the salmon cubes and allow to marinate for 20 minutes. Thread the salmon on to 8 pre-soaked wooden skewers.

2   For the slaw, combine the first 6 ingredients and set aside. Whisk together the lime juice, honey and soy sauce to make the dressing.

3   Heat a large non-stick frying pan to very hot, add the skewers and cook on all 4 sides for 1 minute each. Baste with the marinade during cooking. Keep warm.

4   Combine the salad with enough of the dressing to coat, and divide between 4 plates. Top each salad pile with 2 salmon skewers.

Also try

- Any of the meaty fishes, such as tuna or swordfish, can replace the salmon.

- Some children resist cabbage in their early years, so you could substitute some other blanched vegetables: mangetout, broccoli florets, cauliflower florets, sugar-snap peas etc.

Honey-mustard chicken

How simple is this? Throw it together and serve with a smile
and a huge bowl of mixed vegetables.

Serves 4

8 free-range chicken thighs
2 tbsp whole-grain mustard
2 tbsp runny honey
salt and ground black pepper

1   Preheat the oven to 190°C/375°F/gas mark 5.

2   Put the chicken thighs in a roasting tin in a single layer.

3   Mix together the mustard and honey, season with salt and
    ground black pepper to taste, and brush the mixture all
    over the chicken thighs.

4   Cook in the preheated oven for 20 minutes, brushing the
    chicken with the pan juices occasionally, until the chicken is
    cooked through.

Barbecue jerk chicken

Another way of spicing up chicken, which can be a bland meat.

Serves 4

8 free-range chicken thighs,
  boned
2 tbsp vegetable oil
salad leaves to serve

Marinade
1 tsp ground allspice
1 tsp ground cinnamon
1 tsp dried thyme
¼ tsp freshly grated nutmeg
1 tbsp demerara sugar
2 garlic cloves, crushed
2 tbsp grated onion
1 tbsp red wine vinegar
1 tbsp lime juice
½ tsp chilli powder
salt and ground black pepper

1 Combine all the marinade ingredients in a small bowl. Using a fork, mash them together well to form a thick paste.

2 Lay the chicken pieces on a board and make several lengthways slits in the flesh. Rub the marinade all over the chicken and into the slits.

3 Place the chicken pieces in a dish, cover with clingfilm and leave to marinate overnight in the fridge.

4 Brush off any excess marinade from the chicken. Brush with the oil, and either place on a baking sheet under the grill or on the barbecue. Cook, turning often, on a medium heat for 15-20 minutes, until cooked through.

5 Serve hot with salad leaves.

Also try

● Use salmon instead of chicken, but only marinate for 30 minutes and cook for 10 minutes.

● This is an excellent marinade for pork chops – marinade overnight in the fridge and cook under a high grill for 8-10 minutes on each side, depending on the thickness of the chop.

Chicken tikka

Whenever children start going to the local Indian, this is the best introductory dish, which is also easy to make at home.

Serves 6

1 tsp grated fresh root ginger

1 tsp crushed garlic

½ tsp chilli powder

¼ tsp turmeric

1 tsp salt

150g (5½oz) Greek yoghurt

4 tbsp lemon juice

1 tbsp chopped coriander

12 free-range chicken thighs, skinned, boned and cut into 2½cm (1 inch) cubes

1 tbsp vegetable oil

1 In a medium bowl, combine the ginger and garlic pulp, chilli powder, turmeric, salt, yoghurt, lemon juice and coriander. Fold in the chicken and leave to marinate for at least 2 hours.

2 Place the marinated chicken on a grill tray or in a flameproof dish lined with foil and baste with the vegetable oil.

3 Preheat the grill to medium. Grill the chicken for 15-20 minutes, until cooked, turning and basting several times.

4 Serve garnished with salad and coriander, boiled rice and vegetables.

Also try

- Use fish instead of chicken, but only marinate for 30 minutes and only cook for 10 minutes.

Cheesy chicken gratin crunch

A cheat's leftover dish that can be knocked together in a flash. For children it makes a more acceptable dish than cold chicken and salad.

Serves 4

55g (2oz) unsalted butter

55g (2oz) plain flour

300ml (10fl oz) semi-skimmed milk, warm

300ml (10fl oz) chicken stock, warm

3 tbsp Greek yoghurt

85g (3oz) Cheddar cheese, grated

½ tbsp Dijon mustard

1 tbsp Worcestershire sauce

450g (1lb) cooked leftover free-range chicken

175g (6oz) freshly cooked rice

115g (4oz) frozen peas, defrosted

115g (4oz) shop-bought croûtons

1   Preheat the oven to 180°C/350°F/gas mark 4.

2   Melt the butter in a non-stick saucepan, stir in the flour and cook for 3 minutes over a low heat. Gradually add the milk and stock, stirring continuously until the sauce is smooth. Cook gently for 10 minutes, stirring from time to time.

3   Fold in the yoghurt, cheese, mustard and Worcestershire sauce and stir until the cheese has melted. Fold in the chicken, rice and peas, then place in a gratin dish.

4   Top the chicken with the croûtons, pushing them gently into the mix so only half of each croûton is showing. Cook in the preheated oven for 20-25 minutes, until bubbling. Lower the heat if the croûtons start to burn.

Also try

- Use leftover boiled bacon instead of chicken.

- Fold in a chopped hard-boiled egg and some different pre-cooked vegetables that may be hanging about in the fridge.

- Use breadcrumbs mixed with Parmesan, parsley and melted butter instead of croutons.

Melting cheese, ham and sweet chilli quesadillas

A hot 'sandwich' that's hard to resist, very quick to make and teasingly tempting, one of those moreish sandwiches that normally require you to prepare second helpings.

Serves 4

8 soft flour tortillas
115g (4oz) Emmental or Gruyère cheese, grated
115g (4oz) cooked ham or 55g (2oz) Parma ham, thinly sliced
½ tsp very finely chopped sage leaves
2 tbsp sweet chilli sauce

1   Heat a 23cm (9 inch) non-stick frying pan. Place 1 tortilla in the bottom, then top with a quarter of the grated cheese, leaving a 1cm (½ inch) border all round.

2   Arrange a quarter of the ham on top of the cheese, sprinkle with a little of the sage and drizzle with sweet chilli sauce. Top with a second tortilla and cook for about 1 minute.

3   Invert a large plate on top of the frying pan and turn over so the tortilla is now on the plate. Slide it back into the pan and cook for a further minute. Slide on to a plate and keep warm while cooking the other 3 tortillas. (The sandwiches can be constructed ahead and cooked in a 180°C/350°F/gas mark 4 oven for 6-8 minutes, but the texture of the tortilla will not be quite as nice.)

4   Cut each *quesadilla* into wedges.

Also try

- Use cooked bacon instead of ham.

- Sliced tomatoes make a healthy extra layer.

Pasta with pancetta and peas

Children love pasta, most like peas and I don't know many who turn up their noses to bacon, so put them all together and what do you get? A family favourite.

Serves 4

400g (14oz) dried pasta, such as penne

salt and cracked black pepper

300g (10oz) frozen peas

25g (1oz) unsalted butter

4 tbsp olive oil

1 onion, finely diced

12 slices pancetta or smoked streaky bacon, cut into strips

2 tbsp finely chopped mint leaves

1 tbsp chopped flat-leaf parsley

55g (2oz) Parmesan, freshly grated

1 Place the pasta in a large saucepan of lightly salted water and cook for 10-12 minutes, or until *al dente*. While it is cooking, place the peas in boiling water and blanch for 2 minutes, then drain.

2 Heat a frying pan over a medium to high heat. Add the butter, oil, onion and pancetta and cook for 6 minutes, until the pancetta is crisp. Then add the peas and cook for a further 3 minutes. Drain the pasta, then add to the peas and toss to combine.

3 In a large serving bowl, toss the pasta with the mint, parsley, Parmesan and pepper. Serve immediately.

Also try

- Add other blanched green vegetables.

- A few chilli flakes added to the onion mix give a little kick.

Lamb chops with a mint jelly crust

More of an idea than a recipe, this is another way of introducing children to new flavours.

Serves 4

8 lamb chops, about 115g (4oz) each

salt and ground black pepper

1 tbsp Dijon mustard

55g (2oz) fresh white breadcrumbs

2 tbsp mint jelly

1 tbsp melted butter

1   Preheat the oven to 190°C/375°F/gas mark 5.

2   Place the lamb chops on a baking sheet and season with salt and ground black pepper. Paint the top of the chops with Dijon mustard.

3   Put the breadcrumbs, mint jelly and butter in a bowl and mix together to combine. Spoon the breadcrumb mixture on top of the chops, pressing down firmly with the back of a spoon, making sure they stick to the chops.

4   Bake the chops in the preheated oven for 20 minutes, or until they are just cooked through. Serve immediately.

Also try

● Use redcurrant jelly instead of mint jelly.

Weekend dinners

For most of us the weekend is a time when the family gets together. I particularly look forward to sitting down at the dinner table with everyone. I hate the idea of children coming in at different times of the day and demanding food as if home were an à la carte restaurant. That's never going to happen in the Worrall Thompson household! We can work around the kids' sporting activities, parties and the like, but once meal times at weekends are set they are sacrosanct, and we have compulsory attendance.

On Saturdays and Sundays, most of us have the time to spend a little longer preparing our family meals. More and more men are getting into the kitchen, where cooking can be a relaxing diversion from the rigours of weekday life. It's a good idea to use the time to get the kids helping with the shopping and cooking too. They can learn as they go along, and most kids are much happier to eat food that they have helped to prepare themselves.

When planning a lunch or dinner, try and think seasonally. Fresh ingredients taste so much better when they haven't travelled thousands of miles from some overseas clime. Try to shop at farmer's markets and farm shops, and encourage the kids to ask the farmer or seller questions about how the food is grown and where it comes from. Shopping can be a good opportunity to teach them about the kind of farms that are near your home and the issues surrounding good and bad farming practices.

The weekend meal is a great time for the family to talk about the events of the previous week. With luck, laughter will predominate, but this can also be a time for the kids to tell you about any problems they have. It's a chance for you to really get to know them and find out what kind of week they've had. As parents, you probably have temptations and invitations of your own that can distract you from spending time with your children and teaching them to care about others. So make the most of these special times. After all, togetherness doesn't happen in front of a TV or computer screen.

'The weekend meal is a great time for the family to talk about the events of the previous week.'

Roast loin of pork with apple sauce

My children's favourite Sunday lunch, especially when made with rare breed pork. Serve with roasted root vegetables, a green vegetable and roast potatoes.

Serves 8-10

1 x 2.25kg (5lb) pork loin on the
  bone, skin lightly scored
  at 5mm (¼ inch) intervals
2 tbsp cider vinegar
1 tbsp olive oil
2 tbsp coarse sea salt
8 fresh bay leaves
8 garlic cloves, unpeeled
3 fresh sage leaves
1 red onion, cut into wedges
600ml (1 pint) fresh chicken stock
  (from a carton is fine)

Apple sauce
900g (2lb) Bramley cooking
  apples, peeled, cored and sliced
4-5 tbsp cold water
juice of ½ lemon
1 tbsp caster sugar
55g (2oz) unsalted butter, cut into
  cubes
salt and ground black pepper

1   Put the pork, skin-side down, on a chopping board and trim any loose fat or connective tissue. Put it on a wire rack in the kitchen sink, then pour a kettle of boiling water over the rind, leave for 30 seconds, allow to drain, then repeat 2-3 times. Pour over the vinegar and massage into the skin. Transfer to a plate and leave uncovered in the bottom of the fridge overnight.

2   Preheat the oven to 220°C/425°F/gas mark 7. Place the pork in a roasting tin and drizzle over the oil, massaging it into the skin. Sprinkle over the salt and roast for 30 minutes, then reduce the temperature to 190°C/375°F/gas mark 5 and cook for another hour. Add the bay, garlic, sage and onion, tossing to coat them in the juices. Cook for a further hour, or until the pork is completely tender and the crackling crispy.

3   Meanwhile, place the apples in a pan with the water and lemon juice. Cook over low heat for 12-15 minutes, until the apples have softened, stirring occasionally. Stir in the sugar and whisk in the butter, then keep warm. Spoon into a bowl.

4   When the pork is cooked, transfer to a large platter and leave to rest in a warm place for 10-15 minutes. Put the roasting tin directly on the hob and deglaze it with a little stock, scraping the bottom with a wooden spoon to remove any sediment. Pour in the remaining stock, increase the heat and simmer until the liquid has reduced by half. Season, then strain into a gravy boat and skim off any excess fat.

5   Cut through the fat of the joint just underneath the crackling to remove it in one piece, then cut into portions. Carve the pork into slices and plate them up with vegetables and roast potatoes. Serve with gravy and warm apple sauce.

Also try

- For a cold apple sauce, leave out the butter.

Pot-roast bacon with sticky dried fruits

Bacon joints and slices are always a favourite in our household, especially with my wife being Irish. This dish smacks of the Christmas glazed ham, but it's good all year round.

Serves 4-6

1kg (2¼lb) bacon joint (rind on)
fresh cherries, to garnish
 (optional)

Marinade
115g (4oz) dried cherries
115g (4oz) dried cranberries
115g (4oz) dried apricots, diced
115g (4oz) mustard fruits (see
 below)
2 tbsp dark muscovado sugar
1 tsp salt
½ tsp ground black pepper
6 bay leaves
4 garlic cloves, crushed to a paste
 with salt
2 tbsp quince paste (membrillo)
2 tbsp extra virgin olive oil
150ml (5fl oz) dry white wine
 (optional)
150ml (5fl oz) sherry or balsamic
 vinegar
300ml (10fl oz) chicken stock

1   For the marinade, combine the dried and mustard fruits with the sugar, salt, pepper and bay leaves. Mash together the garlic and quince paste then whisk in the olive oil, wine if using (if not add an extra 150ml stock), vinegar and stock.

2   Combine the fruits with the liquid, then add the bacon joint. Marinate overnight, ideally, or for at least 3-4 hours, basting from time to time.

3   Preheat the oven to 180°C/350°F/gas mark 4.

4   Transfer the bacon, fruits and marinade to a flameproof casserole, place on the hob and bring to the boil. Cover with a lid, then place in the preheated oven for 1¼ hours, basting from time to time.

5   Remove the bacon joint from the casserole and allow to rest for 15 minutes. Meanwhile, place the juices and fruits on the hob and simmer until the sauce is thick and sticky.

6   Remove the rind from the bacon and return the joint to the sauce to glaze for 5 minutes, basting continuously.

7   Serve on a platter, garnished with fresh cherries if available, with new potatoes or mashed potatoes and some buttered cabbage or peas.

Also try

- Substitute duck or pork for the ham, but brown them both all over before starting to cook.

- Mostarda di Cremona, or mustard fruits, are an Italian speciality. Fruits are candied in a strongly mustard-flavoured sugar syrup, and they are available in good Italian delicatessens. If unavailable, increase the quantities of the other fruits.

Dublin coddle

'Coddling' means slow cooking, and this slow-cooked dish is wonderful winter comfort food. I married my Dublin wife, Jacinta, hoping she would cook this dish (it wasn't the only reason), but unfortunately she had never experienced the delights. This typical dish of bacon, sausages and potatoes originates from the 17th century. I have since added cabbage – sorry Dublin!

Serves 8

1kg (2¼lb) unsmoked bacon joint, soaked in cold water overnight

450g (1lb) pork and leek sausages

450g (1lb) onions, sliced

1kg (2¼lb) potatoes, peeled and diced

1 tsp soft thyme leaves

½ tsp ground white pepper

½ tsp dry mustard powder

4 tbsp chopped flat-leaf parsley

½ Savoy cabbage, chopped

2 bay leaves

up to 1 litre (1¾ pints) chicken stock

55g (2oz) unsalted butter, cut in small cubes

1   Preheat the oven to 170°C/325°F/gas mark 3.

2   Cut the bacon joint into 5cm (2 inch) pieces. Cut each sausage into 4 pieces.

3   Combine the onions, potatoes, thyme, pepper, mustard, parsley, cabbage and bay leaves.

4   In a deep casserole, make several layers with the bacon, sausages and potato mix, ending with a layer of the potatoes. Pour over enough stock to come level with the final layer of potatoes. Dot with the butter cubes.

5   Place the casserole over a medium heat and bring to a simmer. Cover and place in the preheated oven for about 2 hours, or until the bacon is tender.

6   If required, increase the oven temperature and remove the lid for the last 30 minutes to brown the top layer. This step would not be considered traditional in Dublin. Serve with wedges of soda bread.

Also try

- Use lean lamb neck chops instead of bacon.

- Halve the stock and replace with double cream for a richer dish.

Leg of lamb tagine

Maybe this dish sounds too adventurous for children, but when you think that they love dishes like sweet and sour chicken, the sweetness in this tagine will be quite appealing. Together with the fruit, this makes a good alternative to the traditional Sunday roast.

Serves 6

1 x 2.25kg (5lbs) leg of lamb, knuckle removed

4 tbsp olive oil

1 head garlic, all but 3 cloves crushed to a paste with a little rock salt

1½ tbsp ground black pepper

2 tsp ground cinnamon

3 tsp ground turmeric

1½ tbsp sweet paprika

1 tsp chilli powder

5 onions, blended to a pulp in a food processor

175g (6oz) dried apricots, halved

85g (3oz) flaked almonds, toasted

55g (2oz) sultanas

1 tbsp liquid honey

½ tsp saffron threads, soaked in a little warm water

600ml (1 pint) tomato juice

300ml (10fl oz) lamb or chicken stock

1 x 400g can chopped tomatoes

salt

sprigs of coriander, to serve

1   In a large casserole dish, brown the lamb all over in half the olive oil. Remove and allow to cool. Cut the 3 garlic cloves in thin slices. Make deep incisions all over the lamb, and insert a sliver of garlic in each cut.

2   Combine all the powdered spices with the garlic paste and the remaining olive oil and stir to create a spice rub. Spoon half the rub over the lamb, retaining the other half. Allow the lamb to marinate for at least 2 hours, ideally overnight, covered in the fridge.

3   Preheat the oven to 160-170°C/325°F/gas mark 3. Place the onion pulp in a large casserole and cook gently for 10 minutes with the retained spice mixture, then add the remaining ingredients except the lamb. Bring to the boil, reduce the heat, then add the lamb and cover with a lid.

4   Cook very slowly in the preheated oven for 3 hours, or until the meat wants to part company with the bone with no effort. Remove the leg of lamb to a warmed platter and allow to rest. If the sauce is a little thin, place the casserole on the hob and boil until the sauce is of a coating consistency.

5   Pour the sauce over the lamb, garnish with sprigs of coriander and serve with jewelled couscous (see page 108).

Also try

- Pot-roast chicken tagine using a whole chicken is excellent. Simmer the sauce for half an hour before adding the marinated chicken, then cook, covered, for an hour, depending on the size of the chicken, or until cooked through.

- This works well as a stew using cubed lamb; reduce the cooking time by 45 minutes.

A delicious puff pastry pie

You can put anything you want in this pie. It takes a little weekend effort, but it's very good value and delicious. And children are always impressed with a little effort.

Serves 4

3 onions, finely sliced

55g (2oz) unsalted butter

2 tbsp good olive oil

4 potatoes, peeled and cut into 1cm (½ inch) cubes

225g (8oz) button mushrooms, quartered

1 tsp soft thyme leaves

225g (8oz) pancetta or smoked streaky bacon, cut into thin strips

1 x 300g tub crème fraîche or Greek yoghurt

salt and ground black pepper

450g (1lb) ready-rolled puff pastry

1 free-range egg yolk

1 Cook the onions slowly in the butter and olive oil for about 20 minutes, until very soft.

2 Add the potatoes, mushrooms, thyme and pancetta. Cover with a lid and cook gently for 12 minutes.

3 Stir in the crème fraîche or yoghurt and season to taste, then cook until the cream coats the vegetables and is not too runny. Allow to cool slightly.

4 Preheat the oven to 200°C/400°F/gas mark 6. Cut the pastry into 2 rectangles, one slightly bigger than the other. Place the smaller rectangle on a floured flat oven tray. Arrange the filling in the centre leaving a 2cm (³/₄ inch) border all the way round. Brush this border with water or egg yolk, then lay the larger rectangle over the filling, pinch the edges together and crimp with a fork.

5 Brush the pastry with egg yolk, taking care not to drip it down the sides otherwise the pastry may not rise evenly. Make 2 slashes in the top of the pastry to let the steam escape.

6 Bake in the preheated oven until puffed and golden, about 25-30 minutes. Serve with green vegetables or a salad.

Also try

- Dot the mixture with Gorgonzola cheese.

- Add chicken strips or sliced sausage instead of bacon and cook as per the bacon.

- A layer of cooked spinach is a great addition.

- For the adventurous, make 4 holes in the mixture and crack a small egg in each cavity before covering with pastry.

Pot-roast chicken

One of my children's favourite meals. If only they knew they were eating really healthily with so many vegetables!

Serves 4

1-2 tbsp olive oil

1 x 1.5kg (3lb 5oz) fresh free-range chicken

115g (4oz) smoked streaky bacon, chopped

1 onion, roughly chopped

3 garlic cloves, finely chopped

2 celery sticks, cut into 2.5cm (1 inch) chunks

2 carrots, cut into 2.5cm (1 inch) chunks

12 new potatoes, washed

1 tbsp soft thyme leaves

2 bay leaves

1 x 400g can chopped tomatoes

1 tbsp Worcestershire sauce

900ml (1½ pints) chicken or vegetable stock

225g (8oz) broccoli florets

115g (4oz) frozen peas

a handful of spinach leaves, washed

115g (4oz) frozen baby broad beans

salt and ground black pepper

1 Preheat the oven to 190°C/375°F/gas mark 5.

2 Place a large flameproof casserole dish over a high heat. Add the olive oil and, when hot, add the chicken, turning occasionally until brown all over. Remove and set aside.

3 Add the bacon to the casserole and fry for a few minutes, then add the onion, garlic, celery, carrots, potatoes, thyme and bay leaves. Pour in the chopped tomatoes and add the Worcestershire sauce. Stir, then add the chicken stock.

4 Return the chicken to the casserole dish and bring to the boil. Put the lid on the casserole and cook in the preheated oven for 1 hour.

5 Remove the chicken and set aside, covered with foil, to keep warm. Add the green vegetables to the casserole and cook on the hob for 6 minutes. Season to taste with some salt and pepper.

6 Carve the chicken. Spoon the vegetables and broth into bowls and top with the chicken.

Also try

● This dish tastes good with pheasant. Reduce the cooking time to 30 minutes (depending on the size of the bird).

● The recipe is great with shoulder of lamb. Increase the cooking time to 1½ hours, or until cooked through.

Chicken with lemon and garlic

A good warming casserole, which is best served with a green vegetable such as buttered cabbage cooked with some smoked bacon.

Serves 4

4 tbsp good olive oil

8-10 free-range chicken thighs, boneless (skin on)

salt and ground black pepper

1 large onion, roughly chopped

1 head garlic, cloves separated

2 celery sticks, roughly chopped

2 carrots, roughly chopped

2 sprigs thyme

2 bay leaves

16 small new potatoes

150ml (5fl oz) dry white wine (optional)

1 litre (1¾ pints) chicken stock

juice and finely grated zest of 2 unwaxed lemons

225g (8oz) frozen peas

2 handfuls baby spinach leaves

1. Heat the oil in a big flameproof casserole dish. Season the chicken, then brown all over. Remove and set aside.

2. Add the onion, garlic, celery, carrots, thyme and bay to the oil in the casserole, reduce the heat and cook until the vegetables have started to soften but not browned too much.

3. Place the chicken back in the casserole with the new potatoes, the wine if using, the chicken stock, the lemon zest and half the juice. Bring to the boil, then reduce the heat to the minimum and cover with a lid. Cook for 1 hour.

4. Remove the chicken and potatoes and keep warm. Boil the remaining mixture until you are left with about 500ml (a scant pint). Blend all the remaining vegetables and liquid, removing the bay and thyme first, in a food processor, then pass through a fine sieve. Return this sauce to the pan.

5. Return the chicken and potatoes to the sauce, then add the peas, spinach and remaining lemon juice, and cook for 6 minutes, stirring from time to time. Make sure the chicken is cooked through. Serve piping hot with warm crusty bread to mop up the juices.

Also try

- Many prefer chicken breasts, which is fine, except that I don't think they stay so succulent and juicy.

- Remove the chicken skin if you wish, but leaving it on creates more flavour and stops the chicken from drying out.

- To make the casserole even more healthy, blanch some more green vegetables – broccoli, asparagus, broad beans, sugar-snap peas etc – and add them just before serving.

- Add a drained rinsed 400g can of white cannellini beans instead of peas.

An exciting fish hot-pot

Another dish to bring your children to greater culinary heights. My two are very receptive to shellfish. The kids are fascinated by the structure of the dish, sucking on the shellfish, potatoes that have changed flavour and that interesting hit of chilli. Serve with toasted baguette slices rubbed with a raw garlic clove.

Serves 4

3 tbsp good olive oil

2 onions, finely chopped

4 garlic cloves, crushed to a paste
  with a little sea salt

½ tsp dried chilli flakes

2 bay leaves

½ tsp ground fennel

2 strips fresh or dried orange peel

a pinch of saffron threads, soaked
  in a little warm water

2 x 400g cans chopped tomatoes

4 medium floury potatoes, peeled
  and quartered

1kg (2¼lb) mussels, cleaned and
  beards removed

450g (1lb) white fish, such as cod,
  haddock, hake or monkfish,
  skinned, boned and cut into
  2.5cm (1 inch) chunks

8 large raw prawns, peeled

salt and ground black pepper

1 Heat the olive oil in a large saucepan. Add the onions, garlic and chilli flakes, and cook gently for 8-10 minutes, without colouring. Add the bay leaves, ground fennel, orange peel and saffron with its liquid, and cook for 2 minutes.

2 Add the tomatoes and potatoes and cook for 12-15 minutes until the potatoes are tender.

3 Meanwhile, check the mussels – discard any that are damaged, or that do not close when tapped against the side of the sink. Add the white fish and cook for 4 minutes, then add the shellfish and cook until the mussels open – a couple of minutes only.

4 Remove the orange peel and bay leaves and any mussels that remain closed before serving. Season to taste and serve piping hot.

Also try

- If you want the dish to be soupier, add a glass of dry white wine after the onions have softened or, if alcohol is not for you, add 300ml (10fl oz) fish stock.

- Use prepared clams instead of mussels and add some squid rings at the same time as the shellfish when you feel the children are ready to expand their horizons.

Salt

We are currently being advised to almost halve our daily salt consumption. While this may be no bad thing, there is no conclusive evidence that salt damages our health. We all know that we shouldn't give babies salt and that young children should have a limited amount, but we really don't know how much adults should consume.

As with many foods we eat, our required salt intake is influenced by the amount of exercise we take. If we sweat, we lose salt and it needs to be replaced; if we are couch slouches or sofa loafers, we don't need much salt, so a more careful balancing act is required.

Nevertheless, it seems clear that we would all benefit from reducing our salt consumption. One way to do this is to season food during cooking rather than that very British habit of smothering everything with salt when it comes to the table. There is some debate about whether the salting of cooking water affects the flavour of the vegetables cooked in it. I've tested this on several occasions and find a definite taste difference. I have often said that the difference between a good cook and a poor cook is in the seasoning, and I stand by that.

We do love salt; it is a flavour enhancer and we are conditioned to love the taste of salty snacks. But it doesn't need to be this way; we can wean ourselves off so much of it. Over the last year or so, I have cut back on the amount of salt that I add to food, often by replacing it with spices or even salt substitutes such as seaweed extract. Spices used wisely are a great substitute for salt, as are, in the right application, lemon juice, onions, garlic and herbs.

The key, as with fat and sugar, is to read the labels. You'll be surprised by how much salt is used in the most innocent of foods such as cereals, breads and ready-meals. And remember, where the manufacturer quotes sodium levels, you must multiply them by two-and-a-half times to discover the salt content.

'Our required salt intake is influenced by the amount of exercise we take. If we sweat we lose salt and it must be replaced.'

Salmon baked in foil with citrus juices and dill

This is a fabulous dish which can be cooked in a hot oven or on top of the barbie. The citrus juices help the children accept the earthy taste of the salmon.

Serves 6

6 mandarins or clementines

2 thin-skinned unwaxed lemons

2 shallots

3 tbsp olive oil

4 navel oranges, top and tail removed, each cut in 3 horizontal slices

2 tbsp caster sugar

1 tbsp green peppercorns

1 small bunch dill, roughly chopped

1 side of salmon, filleted, pin-boned and skinned

1 Place the mandarins and lemons in a saucepan big enough to hold them in one layer. Cover the fruit with a plate, then cover the fruit and plate with water. Bring to the boil, reduce the heat and simmer for 1¼ hours. After 45 minutes, remove the plate and add the shallots. Drain and allow to cool.

2 Meanwhile, heat a large frying pan with 1 teaspoon of olive oil until almost smoking. Place the navel orange slices flat in the pan and cook until one side is dark brown. Turn over and repeat, then sprinkle with the caster sugar.

3 Roughly chop the boiled citrus mixture and remove any pips. Place it in a food processor with the peppercorns and dill and blend until almost smooth. Tip into a bowl and set aside.

4 On a work surface, lay out a sheet of foil 25cm (10 inches) longer than the salmon, dull side up. Lightly oil the foil, then lay the caramelized oranges two rows deep and the length of the salmon. Top with the fish. Spoon the clementine, pepper and dill mix on top of the fish, then bring the foil together to create an airtight parcel. Leave to marinate in the fridge for 1 hour. Preheat the oven to 220°C/425°F/gas mark 7.

5 Place the salmon parcel on a flat roasting tray and bake for 15 minutes. Open in front of family and friends so they can enjoy the aroma. Serve with green beans and new potatoes.

Also try

- Bake individual parcels from single portions of fish, such as trout, cod or monkfish.

- Add some oil to the mandarin shallot mix to make an excellent citrus relish to serve with grilled fish or chicken.

Luxury fish pie

Seems like a lot of ingredients, but it makes one heck of a good pie and is always most welcome in our house.

Serves 6-8

Mashed potato

1kg (2¼lb) floury potatoes such
  as Maris Piper, cut into chunks
salt and ground black pepper
55g (2oz) unsalted butter

Fish filling

450ml (16fl oz) semi-skimmed milk
150ml (5fl oz) double cream
2 bay leaves
1 clove
a pinch of freshly grated nutmeg
325g (11½oz) each salmon fillet
  and smoked haddock fillet, each
  in one piece
225g (8oz) raw tiger prawns,
  peeled and deveined

Sauce and topping

55g (2oz) unsalted butter
1 onion, finely diced
55g (2oz) plain flour
4 free-range eggs, hard-boiled
1 tsp anchovy essence
2 tbsp chopped flat-leaf parsley
½ tsp soft thyme leaves
1 tsp dry English mustard powder
55g (2oz) Gruyère cheese, grated
25g (1oz) Parmesan, freshly grated

1 Preheat the oven to 200°C/400°F/gas mark 6. Put the potatoes in a pan of boiling salted water, cover and simmer for 15-20 minutes, or until tender. Drain and return to the pan for 2 minutes to dry out, shaking the pan occasionally. Mash them, then beat in the butter and season.

2 Meanwhile put the milk in a pan with the cream, bay, clove and nutmeg. Add the fish and poach for 6-8 minutes, or until just cooked. In the last minute of cooking, add the prawns. Using a fish slice, transfer the fish and prawns to a plate until cool enough to handle, then flake the flesh, discarding the skin and any bones. Set aside. Strain the poaching liquid and set aside.

3 For the sauce, melt the butter in a large non-stick pan. Add the onion and cook for 6-8 minutes, until it has softened but not coloured, stirring occasionally. Stir in the flour and cook for 3 minutes, stirring. Pour in the poaching liquid a little at a time, whisking after each addition. Once all the liquid is added, reduce the heat and simmer gently for 10 minutes, stirring occasionally, until slightly reduced and thickened.

4 Chop up the eggs. Stir them into the sauce with the anchovy essence, parsley, thyme and mustard powder. Fold in the reserved fish, then season. Leave to cool, then fold in the prawns.

5 Spoon into an ovenproof 2.25 litre (4 pint) dish, then cover with the mash. Spread evenly with a palette knife, then fluff up with a fork. Sprinkle the cheeses over the top, then bake for 30-35 minutes, or until bubbling and golden.

Also try

- Mussels, cleaned, prepared, cooked in a little white wine and shelled, make a good addition. Replace some of the milk with the mussel cooking liquor.

- Children are fond of a few peas or button mushrooms in the pie.

Vegetables

Vegetables – the bane of most parents lives. How do we get our kids to eat their veg? It's no easy task these days.

Why do we struggle with this so much? Is it the guilt factor – worried that we're not good parents, perhaps because we both work, we feel we have to compensate by agreeing to our children's demands? Is it political correctness gone mad – we feel we shouldn't discipline or control them? Is it peer pressure – their friends don't eat vegetables, so why should they? Or could it be that we're just too lazy – we haven't got the patience to hang around waiting for the children to eat their vegetables which, by the time they are eaten, are cold and unattractive?

For parents of teenagers it's not going to be easy to make a new start, but it's less difficult for parents of youngsters. Don't give in; you're the one who's in control. Take stock of what you're giving them.

The 'yuk' factor usually comes into play with cabbage, Brussels sprouts, spinach, broad beans, swede, turnip, mushrooms and sometimes tomatoes – but what about red and green peppers, aubergine, courgettes, asparagus, parsnips and the like? There's a host of fabulous vegetables just waiting for your imagination to run riot.

'But how do I change the habits of a lifetime?', I hear you ask. Be strong, take control, use your imagination – resort to bribery, try camouflaging vegetables, anything! But the real key is to make mealtimes fun, a time to look forward to rather than to fear – there are lots of ideas for doing this later in this chapter.

It is said to take 17 experiences of the same food for a child to get used to it, so you have to persist. Don't take 'no' for an answer. It's a bit like any rule in life: we kick up a fuss in the beginning, then eventually it becomes the norm. Start the kids with very small portions, mix different vegetables together, slip some cabbage or spinach into a soup, wrap some asparagus in bacon, smuggle lots of vegetables into a stew, shepherd's pie or a risotto and, where possible, introduce them to their own vegetable patch. If they've grown it, they'll eat it – trust me, there's pride at stake.

'It is said to take 17 experiences of the same food for a child to get used to it, so you have to persist.'

Bubble and squeak

This is nursery food at its best, loved by generations of children and adults alike.

Serves 4

55g (2oz) unsalted butter
2 onions, chopped
225g (8oz) cooked potato, mashed
225g (8oz) cooked sliced Savoy or
 green cabbage
salt and ground black pepper
1 tbsp beef dripping

1 Melt the butter in a non-stick frying pan and cook the onions over a medium heat until softened but not brown, about 8 minutes.

2 Fold the mash, cabbage and buttery onions together. Season with salt and plenty of pepper. Combine everything thoroughly.

3 In the same pan that you cooked the onions in, melt the dripping and tip in the potato mix. Push the mix down to make a circular cake. Cook for 10 minutes over a medium heat without disturbing. Turn the cake over either by tossing or sliding it on to a plate and then returning it to the pan. It should cook for a further 10 minutes.

4 Serve with grills, or as a dish in its own right with poached eggs and crispy bacon.

Also try

- Originally this dish was made with leftover roast beef as well; you may well want to do the same.

- If you want to reduce the level of saturated fat, replace dripping with 1 tbsp olive oil.

Jewelled couscous

A pleasant accompaniment to a tagine and a whole host of other meats and fish.

Serves 6-8

600ml (1 pint) chicken or
vegetable stock
500g (1lb 2oz) couscous
finely grated zest of 1 unwaxed
lemon
6 tbsp extra virgin olive oil
55g (2oz) flaked almonds, toasted
115g (4oz) ready-to-eat dried
apricots, chopped
55g (2oz) sultanas
2 heaped tbsp chopped flat-leaf
parsley
2 heaped tbsp chopped coriander
salt and ground black pepper

1 Heat the stock in a pan until boiling, then remove from the heat. Pour in the couscous in a thin, steady stream, and then stir in the lemon zest. Cover with clingfilm and set aside for 5 minutes to allow the grains to swell. Remove the clingfilm and fluff up the grains with a fork so that they separate.

2 Return the couscous to the heat and drizzle over the olive oil. Cook gently for a few minutes, stirring with the fork to fluff up the grains, then remove from the heat. You could also do this in a large steamer, lined with a piece of muslin or a couple of new J-cloths. Fold in the almonds, apricots, sultanas, parsley and coriander and season to taste.

3 Tip the couscous into an ovenproof dish, cover with clingfilm and chill until ready to serve. Or you can keep it warm in the bottom of a moderate oven, covered with foil, for up to half an hour until ready to serve. Alternatively, reheat by piercing the clingfilm all over with a fork and heat on high in the microwave for 2-3 minutes or according to manufacturer's instructions. Serve at once.

Also try

Replace the nuts and dried fruit with...

● Sun-dried tomatoes and pesto.

● Lemon zest and poppy seeds.

● Diced blanched vegetables.

Vegetable risotto

This is an excellent way of getting children to eat their veg, as they seem to enjoy rice dishes. There is a little preparation in dicing the vegetables small, their size helps to camouflage them!

Serves 4

1 litre (1¾ pints) vegetable or
   chicken stock, hot
75ml (2½fl oz) good olive oil
2 onions, finely chopped
1 tsp soft thyme leaves
2 garlic cloves, finely chopped
375g (13oz) arborio rice
2 leeks, washed and shredded
2 carrots, peeled and cut into
   1cm (½ inch) dice
2 potatoes, peeled and cut into
   1cm (½ inch) dice
115g (4oz) frozen peas
3 tomatoes, seeded and diced
2 handfuls baby spinach, washed
55g (2oz) Parmesan, grated
55g (2oz) unsalted butter
   (optional)
1 tbsp mascarpone cheese
   (optional)
salt and ground black pepper

1 In a large saucepan, heat the oil, then add the onions, thyme and garlic and cook gently for 8-10 minutes, until the onions have softened without colour.

2 Add the rice, leeks, carrots and potatoes and stir well to coat with the olive oil. Cook for 3 minutes, stirring regularly.

3 Begin to add the hot stock, ladle by ladle. Add more stock when the last ladle has been absorbed. During this time, stir continuously over a moderate to high heat.

4 When the risotto is nearly ready, after about 16 minutes from the time you started adding the stock, fold in the peas, tomatoes and spinach with another ladle of stock. Cook until the spinach has wilted.

5 When the risotto is ready, the rice should be tender but not too soft. The consistency should be slightly soupy so that when you ladle the risotto into a bowl there is a little movement rather than a firm stodge.

6 Just before serving, fold in the Parmesan, butter and mascarpone, if using. Season to taste and serve immediately.

Also try

- A little *pancetta* or diced smoked streaky bacon can be added at the same time as the onions.

- Diced raw chicken breast could be added halfway through cooking – make sure it is cooked through.

- Play with different vegetables, remembering to add any green ones towards the end of cooking to preserve the colour.

- Substitute 225g (8oz) mushrooms for leeks and omit the carrots.

Making mealtimes with kids fun

When my children, Toby and Billie, were young we played games with food. A favourite was the guessing game, which involved blindfolding them and then feeding them different foods while they guessed what they were eating. This, as you can imagine, involves a fair amount of trust – you need to reassure them that you wouldn't give them something you wouldn't eat yourself.

I gave them a piece of juicy rare meat and then a well-done piece and, you've guessed it, they liked the rare meat better. Ever since then, much to the surprise of restaurant waiters, they have ordered their steak or burgers rare or medium-rare. This surprised my wife, Jacinta, too because when we first met she was definitely a well-done girl; she has now weaned herself on to medium-rare.

I have often said that we would get far more pleasure from our food if we were blind, as our brains wouldn't get biased messages from our eyes… 'er yuk, there's blood on the plate, therefore it must taste disgusting'.

My taste test highlights the senses, awakens the brain and, best of all, increases the knowledge of food. It teaches kids the whole gamut of sensations: sweet, sour, salt and bitter (although I must admit we haven't tried out the fifth taste bud, umami).

I might give them a raw carrot, then a cooked one, to help them appreciate texture in food. To explain how mint is used, I would give them toothpaste, chewing gum, chocolate mint, mint imperial, mint sauce and then the real thing, a mint leaf. I would give a green tomato, then a red one (in season, not forced), or a green and red pepper, so they could understand the benefits of the sun and its power to ripen.

I would give them plain boiled cabbage (yuk), then cabbage blanched and tossed with some home-cooked onion, bacon and a hint of fennel seed ('wow, that's delicious'). Mealtimes need to be fun. You can teach your kids manners later – the main thing is to build their confidence, get them into a routine, and the target… to get them not to say 'ah Mum, Dad, do we have to eat this?'.

'My taste test highlights the senses, awakens the brain and, best of all, increases the knowledge of food.'

Potato, onion and Gorgonzola bake

This is a lovely potato dish, perfect to serve with roast or grilled meats. It's best made in large quantities so that it can also be reheated on another occasion.

Serves 6-8

85g (3oz) unsalted butter

8 medium potatoes, peeled and
cut into 3mm (⅛ inch) slices

4 onions, thinly sliced

3 bay leaves

1 tsp soft thyme leaves

2 tbsp chopped parsley

175g (6oz) Gorgonzola cheese,
crumbled

salt and ground black pepper

175ml (6fl oz) dry white wine

175ml (6fl oz) chicken or
vegetable stock

4 tbsp good olive oil

1   Preheat the oven to 200°C/400°F/gas mark 6. Using about 25g (1oz) of the butter, lightly grease a 25 x 5cm (10 x 2 inch) deep gratin dish.

2   Lay half the potato slices over the bottom of the dish, scatter over the onion slices, then dot with the bay leaves. Scatter with the thyme and parsley and dot with Gorgonzola. Season with salt and pepper.

3   Arrange the remaining potatoes over the top; overlap the top layer of potatoes to make a pattern. Pour over the wine and stock (or replace the wine and use all the stock), dot with the remaining butter and sprinkle with the olive oil.

4   Cover the dish with lightly oiled foil, then cook in the preheated oven for 40 minutes. Remove the foil and cook for a further 20 minutes to crisp up the top.

Also try

- Halve the amount of onions and replace with sliced mushrooms or ideally porcini or ceps.

- Halve the amount of onions and add a layer of sliced tomatoes.

- Halve the amount of onions and add frozen peas or a layer of cooked spinach.

- Mix the onion with slices of pancetta or prosciutto.

Vegetable stir-fry

Once a week the children know they have to 'endure' a vegetable-only dinner, so I make it as appetizing as possible.

Serves 4

1 tbsp hoisin sauce

1 tbsp light soy sauce

2 tbsp sweet chilli sauce

2 tbsp sesame oil

2 tbsp vegetable oil

1 carrot, very thinly sliced

1 red pepper, seeded and cut into
  2.5cm (1 inch) squares

115g (4oz) button mushrooms,
  quartered

1 onion, roughly chopped

225g (8oz) mixed green
  vegetables (e.g. broccoli florets,
  baby spinach and thinly sliced
  sugar-snap peas and leeks)

5 tbsp water

2 tsp cornflour

toasted sesame seeds to garnish

1   Whisk together the first 4 ingredients and set aside for the Oriental glaze.

2   Heat the vegetable oil in a wok or frying pan. Add the carrot, pepper, mushrooms and onion and stir-fry over a moderate heat for 5 minutes. Add the green vegetables, increase the heat and cook for 2 minutes, stirring constantly.

3   Pour in the Oriental glaze with 3 tbsp of the water, and cook for 2 minutes.

4   Combine the remaining water with the cornflour to make a smooth paste. Add to the vegetables, bring to the boil and cook for 1 minute.

5   Serve with some fried rice or noodles and sprinkle with sesame seeds.

Also try

- Use whatever vegetables you have to hand, so long as they can be cooked in the time.

- Pre-cook some rice or noodles and fold into the vegetables.

Mediterranean carrot rolls

This dish is exceptionally popular with my children, making a nice supper dish as well as a vegetable side dish.

Serves 4-6

10 medium carrots, cooked until soft and drained

2 slices white bread, rubbed into crumbs

6 organic dried apricots, finely diced

2 tsp chopped sultanas

4 spring onions, finely diced

3 tbsp pine nuts, chopped

4 garlic cloves, finely chopped

1 tsp chilli flakes

2 tsp finely grated unwaxed orange zest

1 free-range egg

6 tbsp mixed chopped parsley, mint and dill

salt and ground black pepper

plain flour for dusting

vegetable oil for shallow-frying

1   Mash the carrots, then add all the remaining ingredients and knead well. If the mixture is too wet, add further breadcrumbs; the mixture should be soft and slightly damp.

2   Mould the purée into about 12 x 5cm (2 inch) cylinders or flat patties, coating your hands with flour to stop them sticking. Roll each piece in flour, then shallow-fry in oil until brown on all sides.

3   Drain well on kitchen paper and serve with salad or as an accompaniment to grilled foods.

Also try

- Roast some pumpkin or butternut squash with a little olive oil, thyme and garlic, and use instead of the carrots.

Cabbage griddle cakes

Cabbage is never the easiest vegetable to encourage children to eat, but here's a recipe that may change that. Serve with either a poached egg and hollandaise, grilled meats or crispy bacon.

Serves 4-6

450g (1lb) Savoy cabbage, shredded
salt and ground black pepper
2 free-range eggs
1 free-range egg yolk
½ onion, grated
125ml (4fl oz) semi-skimmed milk
225g (8oz) plain flour
75g (3oz) unsalted butter, melted
2 tbsp snipped chives
olive oil for frying

1 Cook the cabbage in boiling salted water until tender, about 6-8 minutes. Drain and, when cool enough to handle, pat dry with kitchen paper.

2 Combine the eggs, egg yolks, onion, milk, flour, melted butter and some seasoning in a food processor and blend until smooth. The mixture should have a batter consistency. If too thin, add a little more flour; too thick, a little more milk.

3 Fold the cabbage, chives and some more seasoning into the batter.

4 Heat 1 tbsp of oil in a frying pan and spoon in dollops of cabbage batter. Cook a few at a time, until golden on both sides. Keep warm while cooking a further batch, adding more oil to the pan if necessary.

Also try

- Use any chopped green vegetable instead of cabbage.

Potato, pancetta and Parmesan bake

A simple dish that ups the tempo, incorporating tastes and textures that children love.

Serves 4

2 tbsp garlic-infused olive oil
450g (1lb) waxy potatoes, peeled
  and very thinly sliced
salt and ground black pepper
6 pancetta slices, about 5mm
  (¼ inch) thick
55g (2oz) Parmesan, freshly
  grated

1　Preheat the oven to 180°C/350°F/gas mark 4. Brush a 20cm (8 inch) ovenproof dish with some of the oil.

2　Arrange one-third of the potatoes in the bottom of the dish, season and lay 3 slices of the pancetta over the top. Sprinkle over a little Parmesan and arrange another layer of potatoes on the top.

3　Lay the remaining pancetta on top of the potatoes and sprinkle with a little more Parmesan (reserving a little for use later) and seasoning. Top with the remaining potatoes, season with salt and pepper, and drizzle over the remaining olive oil. Press the potatoes down firmly and cover the dish with foil.

4　Bake in the preheated oven for 30-35 minutes, then uncover and sprinkle with the remaining Parmesan. Bake for a further 15-20 minutes, or until golden.

5　Leave to rest for about 10 minutes, then cut into wedges and serve.

Also try

- Use a mixture of potatoes, parsnips and turnips.

- Use cooked smoked streaky bacon if you can't find pancetta.

Mushroom bread and butter pudding

A savoury take on the classic bread and butter pudding.

Serves 6

2 tbsp vegetable oil

3 red onions, halved and sliced

200g (7oz) button mushrooms, sliced

salt and ground black pepper

40g (1½oz) unsalted butter

6 thin slices white day-old bread, with crusts left on

275g (9½oz) Gruyère cheese, grated

3 free-range eggs

300ml (10fl oz) semi-skimmed milk

300ml (10fl oz) crème fraîche

50g (1¾oz) Parmesan, freshly grated

1 Preheat the oven to 180°C/350°F/gas mark 4. Grease the base of a 20 x 15cm (8 x 6 inch) ovenproof dish.

2 Put the oil into a preheated frying pan. Add the onions and fry gently until golden. Add the mushrooms and pan-fry for a few minutes, until softened and lightly coloured. Season and remove from the heat.

3 Butter the slices of bread and cut each slice into 2 triangles. Cover the base of the greased dish with half of the bread. Scatter over half each of the onion and mushroom mixture and the grated Gruyère. Repeat with the remaining bread, onions, mushrooms and Gruyère.

4 Whisk the eggs, milk, crème fraîche, Parmesan and some seasoning in a large bowl and pour over the top. Allow to rest for an hour.

5 Place the dish inside a roasting dish with warm water to come two-thirds of the way up the sides (a bain-marie), and bake in the preheated oven for 35 minutes until puffy and golden.

6 Serve immediately while the cheese and custard are molten and gooey.

Also try

● Add some fried bacon to the mushroom mix.

● Add a layer of cooked spinach or cabbage.

Baked cheesy broccoli

Here is another way of livening up a vegetable that has become part of the norm in a child's diet.

Serves 4

350g (12oz) cooked broccoli, chopped
3 free-range eggs
350ml (12fl oz) double cream
salt and ground black pepper
85g (3oz) Cheddar or Parmesan, freshly grated

1 Preheat the oven to 180°C/350°F/gas mark 4.

2 Place the chopped cooked broccoli in a small baking dish.

3 Beat the eggs with the double cream, salt and pepper and pour over the broccoli. Sprinkle with cheese.

4 Put in a roasting tray with water to come two-thirds of the way up the sides of the baking dish. Bake in the preheated oven for 45-60 minutes, until the custard is set.

Spicy carrots

Carrots are one of children's favourite vegetables, so it's important to ring the changes or else they may get bored.

Serves 4

450g (1lb) carrots
475ml (17fl oz) water
¼ tsp salt
2 tbsp olive oil
1 large garlic clove, crushed to a paste with a little salt
1 red chilli, seeded and finely chopped
1 tsp ground cumin
1 tsp paprika
juice of 1 lemon
flat-leaf parsley to garnish

1 Cut the carrots into slices 5mm (¼ inch) thick. Bring the water to the boil and add the salt and carrots. Simmer for 10 minutes, until the carrots are just tender. Drain.

2 Gently heat the oil in the pan and toss in the garlic and chilli. Stir over a medium heat for a minute without letting the garlic brown. Stir in the cumin, paprika and lemon juice.

3 Pour the warm mixture over the carrots, tossing well.

4 Spoon into a serving dish and garnish with flat-leaf parsley.

Picnics and barbecues

One of my great memories of childhood is picnics. They offer family entertainment that is affordable and fun. It didn't matter where we ended up – the South Downs, Richmond Park or even at the bottom of the garden – although picnics on the beach didn't work as well; sand in your sandwiches is not a treat!

Picnics were never grand. There were no 4 x 4s with a lowering tailgate door. We had a blanket, a flask and a basket. The food was pretty unimaginative, served from blue plastic containers on blue plastic plates. But it didn't matter, we were spending time with family and friends, and I got used to tinned vegetable salad and sandwich spread sandwiches.

Nowadays we are spoilt for choice. Supermarkets sell Mediterranean vegetables in marinades, sliced meats, dips, crudities... you name it, it is there. And at last we can replace the wicker basket, the quick route to food poisoning, with the Eskie, a chiller box for keeping food cool.

We're fully fledged barbecue cooks these days too. Forget burgers and sausages, there are many great marinades that can turn fish or meat into something special. But beware – there are many cases of food poisoning from barbecues, especially with chicken. The drips of fat fuel the fire and the outside of food can get burnt, leaving the inside raw.

Follow these rules to safe barbecuing:

1 Before you start cooking, have all utensils, condiments, cutlery and a drink for the chef in place.

2 If using charcoal, make sure you light the barbie at least 45 minutes before you start cooking. In sunlight the ashes should look grey and at night have a warm red glow.

3 At night have plenty of light to see what you are cooking.

4 Keep raw and cooked foods apart.

5 Have a water spray at your fingertips to douse the flames.

6 If taking a portable barbie on a picnic, make sure you are not at risk of setting fire to the countryside.

7 For salads of accompaniments, think Mediterranean so you can serve them at room temperature.

8 Don't be drunk in charge of a barbecue.

9 Involve the children as much as possible.

'There are a great many marinades that can turn fish or meat into something special.'

Mediterranean sandwich

This is a fab stuffed loaf, well worth the effort.

Serves 4-6

1 Pugliese loaf (Italian round
  country bread)
1 garlic clove, halved
olive oil for drizzling
4 tbsp tapenade
1 aubergine, sliced and
  char-grilled
30 large basil leaves
140g (5oz) sliced courgette,
  char-grilled
4 tbsp pesto
140g (5oz) sun-dried tomatoes
2 red peppers, char-grilled and
  skinned
2 yellow peppers, char-grilled and
  skinned
4 ready-to-eat slices *mortadella*
  (optional)
400g (14oz) buffalo mozzarella,
  thinly sliced
115g (4oz) stoned black olives,
  coarsely chopped
55g (2oz) red onion, thinly sliced
10 slices Italian salami (optional)
55g (2oz) rocket leaves
55g (2oz) spinach leaves, washed
  and dried
salt and ground black pepper
1 tbsp balsamic vinegar

1   Cut the lid off the top of the loaf and hollow out the bread,
    leaving a crust of about 1.5cm ($^5/_8$ inch) all the way round.

2   Rub the cut surface of the bread and lid with the garlic,
    then drizzle with olive oil. Spread the tapenade on the
    bottom of the loaf, then layer up all the ingredients in the
    order in which they appear in the ingredients list,
    seasoning generously with salt and black pepper between
    each layer. Sprinkle on the vinegar between the rocket and
    spinach leaves.

3   Replace the lid and wrap the loaf in clingfilm. If you want a
    really condensed sandwich, place in the refrigerator and
    leave pressed under a heavy weight overnight.

4   Serve the sandwich in wedges.

Also try

- If you want the sandwich to be vegetarian, simply omit the
  cured meats.

Leek and two-cheese pasties

An excellent vegetarian alternative to the usual meat pasty.

Serves 4

3 tbsp olive oil

25g (1oz) unsalted butter

2 medium onions, finely sliced

4 medium leeks, white and light
   green parts only, sliced

1 garlic clove, crushed

1 tsp soft thyme leaves

1 tbsp plain flour

salt and ground black pepper

200ml (7fl oz) semi-skimmed milk

2 free-range eggs, lightly beaten

115g (4oz) Gruyère cheese, grated

2 tbsp freshly grated Parmesan

1 x 500g packet ready-made
   shortcrust pastry

1 free-range egg, beaten

1   Heat the oil and butter in a saucepan until melted. Add the onions, leeks, garlic and thyme and cook over a low heat for 40 minutes, until the vegetables are meltingly soft and have started to turn golden. Stir the mixture regularly. Allow to cool slightly. Fold in the flour and season to taste.

2   Preheat the oven to 200°C/400°F/gas mark 6.

3   Mix the milk and eggs together, then add to the onion mixture in the pan. Fold in half the Gruyère and half the Parmesan. Cook over a low heat until thickened (do not boil), then allow to cool.

4   Roll out the pastry and cut out 4 x 15cm (6 inch) circles. Divide the leek and cheese mixture among the pastry circles, leaving a 2.5cm (1 inch) gap around the borders. Brush the edges of the circles with beaten egg.

5   Fold each pastry in half so the edges meet, crimp to make a tight seal, then place on a baking sheet. Make 2 small slits in each pasty to allow steam to escape, then brush with beaten egg.

6   Bake in the preheated oven for 25-30 minutes, until golden. Serve hot, warm or at room temperature.

Also try

- Add different vegetables, such as carrots, potatoes, pumpkin or broccoli.

- Add strips of cooked chicken to the onion and leek mix.

Honey, mustard and dill sausages

An all-time favourite, which we serve at The Greyhound and which is always popular at cocktail parties.

Serves 6-8

675g (1½lb) your favourite cocktail sausages
1 tbsp English mustard
3 tbsp grain mustard
25g (1oz) salted butter, softened
2 tbsp finely chopped dill
5 tbsp runny honey

1 Place the sausages in a non-stick frying pan, over a medium heat, for about 8 minutes, or until golden and cooked through.

2 Meanwhile, mix together the mustards, butter, dill and honey, taste and adjust the mixture by adding a little more mustard or honey to your own liking. Heat in a frying pan over a medium heat.

3 Add the sausages to the mustard and dill dressing and toss until glazed and sticky. Serve immediately (making sure you have cocktail sticks and napkins to hand).

Also try

- Adults may prefer to use extra English mustard for more bite.

- Omit the dill if the children aren't ready for a bit of greenery with their picnic food.

A salad of tagliatelle, smoked mackerel and toasted pumpkin seeds

You can rarely go wrong with pasta and children, and this salad should be no different.

Serves 2

3 tbsp olive oil

juice of 1 lemon

salt and ground black pepper

300g (10½oz) tagliatelle, tagliatelle verde, or any other pasta shape

2 fillets smoked mackerel, flaked, or 1 x small can tuna, drained

1 x 10cm (4 inch) chunk cucumber, diced

2 small carrots, grated

4 tbsp pumpkin seeds, toasted

8 cherry tomatoes, halved

1 Little Gem lettuce, shredded

4 radishes, finely sliced

1 Mix the olive oil, lemon juice and a grind of black pepper. Set to one side.

2 Cook the tagliatelle in boiling salted water according to the pack instructions until *al dente*, then drain well. While still warm, toss with the dressing.

3 In a large bowl toss the rest of the ingredients together with the pasta, season and serve at room temperature.

Also try

- Prawns will make this even more protein-packed for energetic little ones or grown-ups alike. Mix in around 55g (2oz) cooked peeled prawns with the rest of the ingredients at the end.

- Use cooked chicken instead of the mackerel.

Inverted cheese burger

There are burgers and there are real burgers. Try this one.

Serves 4

750g (1lb 10oz) minced beef
(18% fat)
1 onion, finely chopped and
gently cooked until soft in a
little unsalted butter
1 free-range egg, beaten
1 tbsp Dijon mustard
4 x 25g (1oz) nuggets of
mozzarella cheese
25g (1oz) Parmesan, freshly
grated
salt and coarsely ground black
pepper
4 burger buns, halved

1 Combine the beef, cooked onion, egg and Dijon mustard
   and mix thoroughly.

2 Roll the mozzarella nuggets in the grated Parmesan.

3 Form the beef into 4 patties. Make a deep indentation in
   each of the burgers and place a nugget of Parmesan-
   mozzarella in each one, folding the beef back around the
   cheese until it is totally sealed. Sprinkle some black pepper
   over each burger and refrigerate until ready to cook.

4 Grill, pan-fry or barbecue the burgers for 4 minutes each
   side for rare, 6 minutes for medium or 8-9 minutes for
   well-done. Season with salt.

5 Toast the cut side of burger buns. Place each burger between
   a cut bun. Serve with coleslaw and oven-cooked chips.

Also try

- Try this with pork or chicken mince with a little grated suet added to
  keep it juicy.

- Place slices of Emmental cheese and crispy cooked bacon on top
  and melt under the grill.

Beef and chicken yakitori

Always popular, these moreish kebabs give an Oriental twist to barbie food. Don't worry about the alcohol content in the marinade, as it burns off during cooking – although you can leave it out if you prefer.

Serves 4

100ml (3½fl oz) *kecap manis* (sweet soy sauce)

3 tbsp rice vinegar

1 tbsp runny honey

4 tbsp mirin (sweet rice wine) or dry sherry

1 tbsp Szechuan peppercorns, ground

2 garlic cloves, crushed to a paste

1 x 1cm (½ inch) piece fresh root ginger, grated

1 tbsp sweet chilli sauce

3 free-range chickens breasts, skinned and cut into 1cm (½ inch) cubes

325g (11½oz) beef fillet or trimmed sirloin, cut into 1cm (½ inch) cubes

1   Combine the first 8 ingredients in a bowl, then fold in the chicken and beef and allow to marinate for 2 hours.

2   Thread 4 pre-soaked wooden skewers with the chicken and do the same with the beef.

3   Char-grill or grill the skewers under a medium heat for 2 minutes on each side of the 4 sides of the chicken and 1 minute on each side for the beef or until they are all cooked through. While the meats are cooking, brush from time to time with a little marinade.

4   Serve with stir-fried vegetables and rice.

Also try

- Pork, lamb, jumbo prawns, salmon, tuna and monkfish also work well, although you would only need to marinate the fish for half an hour and grill each ingredient until cooked through.

- Alternate vegetables between each piece of meat for a more healthy option – cherry tomatoes, button mushrooms, red peppers and onion.

Baked sweet potatoes cooked on coals

Baked sweet potatoes make a great alternative to ordinary jacket potatoes, and cooking them in the coals adds another dimension. Make sure the coals have burnt down to glowing red in darkness or powdery grey in sunlight. I've included a flavoured butter to serve with the potatoes.

Serves 4

4 medium sweet potatoes (red skin, orange flesh)
olive oil, for brushing

Tomato and chilli butter
2 tbsp chopped flat-leaf parsley
2 garlic cloves, roughly chopped
4 sun-dried tomatoes, drained
2 mild chillies, seeded and roughly chopped
2 tsp rosemary leaves
1 tbsp lemon juice
½ tsp Maldon sea salt
250g (9oz) unsalted butter, softened

1 For the butter, combine the first 7 ingredients in a food processor and blend until combined. Add the softened butter and pulse until combined. Wrap in foil and chill.

2 Scrub the sweet potatoes, prick all over with a fork and double wrap in lightly oiled foil. Place in the embers of the barbecue or in the oven (200°C/400°F/gas mark 6) and cook for 1 hour, turning regularly.

3 Cut a cross shape in each potato through the foil and push the 4 corners between the cuts to push out the centres. Pop on a knob of tomato butter, to serve.

Also try

- If oven-roasting the potatoes, don't use foil, just rub the surface of the potatoes with olive oil and a little rock salt if you wish.

● Finger-licking ribs

Who can resist a sticky rib, and these are very sticky indeed...

Serves 4

300ml (10fl oz) tomato ketchup
150ml (5fl oz) dark soy sauce
125g (4½oz) runny honey
1 x 5cm (2 inch) piece fresh root
  ginger, peeled and finely grated
4 garlic cloves, finely chopped
1.8-2.25kg (4-5lb) pork spare ribs,
  still joined

1   Place the tomato ketchup in a large shallow dish with the soy sauce, honey, ginger and garlic, then mix thoroughly to combine. Add the ribs, cover with clingfilm and chill for up to 24 hours if time allows.

2   Place the ribs in a large, deep pan; you may have to cut them in half to get them to fit. Pour over the tomato ketchup mixture and then add enough water to completely cover them. Bring to a simmer, cover, then cook over a medium heat for 45 minutes to 1 hour, until tender.

3   Remove the ribs from the heat and transfer to a large shallow non-metallic dish, then cook the marinade for a further 20 minutes, or until reduced and sticky. When the marinade has cooked, pour over the ribs, cover with clingfilm and chill until ready to grill.

4   Preheat the grill to medium. When you want to use the ribs, carefully scoop off the fat from the top of the mixture and discard, then allow the mixture to come back up to room temperature. Drain all the marinade off the ribs and set it aside.

5   Arrange the ribs on a grill rack and cook for about 8 minutes on each side, basting or painting them with the reduced marinade occasionally.

6   To serve, cut the ribs into single ribs and arrange on a large platter.

Also try

● If using baby back ribs, only cook them in the marinade for half an hour.

● Add a few fennel seeds and chilli flakes to zap up the flavour.

Puddings

Puds and children go together like bread and a sandwich filling; they should not be kept apart. Children deserve puddings. But I need to add a caveat to that statement: as long as children are not couch-slouches or sofa-loafers and they do enough exercise to warrant the extra calories, they deserve puddings.

When I was at school we participated in one-and-a-half hours of sports every single day, and we could eat practically anything that was put in front of us and remain slim. In fact, at the age of 17 I was only 100lb – how things have changed!

We Brits excel at pudding, but most of our classic puds stem from an era when our bodies needed the extra fuel, as our food was designed to help us do physical work and to keep out the cold. With central heating, carpets, double glazing, duvets and a lack of physical activity, the demand for the likes of chocolate puddings, steamed pudding with cornflour sauce, jam roly-poly, spotted dick, bread and butter pudding, sticky toffee pudding and treacle tart – to name but a few of the dishes of my childhood memories – is bound to lessen. This is a pity because these puds are all yummy. But in the name of obesity there's no place for the heavy pudding in an everyday meal for all but the most active of families.

It used to be common to eat a pudding with lunch and to have fruit with supper, but now puddings are consigned to infrequent occasions. However, children musn't be denied them completely. My advice is to keep them on the back burner for that little surprise that will light up their faces.

For everyday suppers, my children get 101 ways with fruit as part of my personal quest to give them 5 vegetables and 2 fruits a day – 2 more portions than the government recommends. But within my hard exterior lies a soft centre, so I do love to treat them from time to time! Everything in moderation should be your by-line – a sensible approach to family food. Only you know your kids' routines and so only you know best how often you can treat them.

'Keep puds on the back burner for that little surprise.'

Apple and mascarpone rice pudding

Almost a sweet risotto, this makes a nice change from bog standard rice pudding.

Serves 4

Apples
25g (1oz) unsalted butter
2 small Granny Smith apples,
    peeled, cored and cut into 1cm
    (½ inch) dice
5 tbsp golden caster sugar
freshly grated nutmeg
a pinch of ground cinnamon
1 tsp vanilla extract

Risotto
600ml (1 pint) unsweetened apple
    juice
600ml (1 pint) semi-skimmed milk
25g (1oz) unsalted butter
300g (10½oz) arborio rice
1 tsp soft thyme leaves
1 bay leaf
175g (6oz) mascarpone cheese
55g (2oz) flake almonds or
    walnuts, toasted and coarsely
    chopped (optional)

1   For the apples, melt the butter in a small, heavy, non-stick frying pan over a medium heat. Add the apples, sugar, nutmeg and cinnamon and cook until the apples are just tender, about 6 minutes. Stir in the vanilla.

2   For the risotto, heat the apple juice and milk in separate saucepans.

3   Melt the butter in a large heavy non-stick saucepan over a medium to low heat. Add the rice, thyme and bay leaf and stir for 2 minutes. Alternately add the hot apple juice, then the hot milk, ladle by ladle, until the liquid has been absorbed and the rice is cooked, about 20 minutes.

4   Stir in the cooked apple mixture and fold in 85g (3oz) of the mascarpone.

5   To serve, divide the rice pudding among 4 plates. Top with the remaining mascarpone, and sprinkle with nuts. Serve immediately.

Also try

- Use pears and sultanas instead of apples.

Blackberry and apple Yorkshire pudding

I remember having this when visiting some relatives in the north, as a young child. My initial thoughts were 'how strange', but when I tasted it with a jug of piping-hot custard, it had a comforting wow factor!

Serves 4

115g (4oz) plain flour

175g (6oz) caster sugar

a pinch of salt

3 free-range eggs, beaten

300ml (10fl oz) semi-skimmed milk

325g (11½oz) Bramley apples, peeled, cored and sliced

115g (4oz) blackberries

finely grated zest of 1 unwaxed lemon

2 tbsp vegetable oil

25g (1oz) unsalted butter

1 Sift the flour, 115g (4oz) of the sugar and the salt into a mixing bowl, make a well in the centre and pour in the eggs and a little milk. With a hand-whisk, gradually draw in the dry ingredients to make a smooth paste, then gradually fold in the remaining milk to make a batter. Allow to rest for half an hour, ideally for a couple of hours.

2 Meanwhile, combine the fruits, remaining sugar and the lemon zest and allow to macerate for half an hour.

3 Preheat the oven to 200°C/400°F/gas mark 6. Take a pie dish, pour in the vegetable oil, swirl to coat and pop in the oven for 8 minutes to preheat.

4 Remove the dish from the oven and add the butter, which will melt instantly. Tip in the fruit, then pour over the stirred batter. Return immediately to the oven and bake for 30 minutes, until well risen, crisp and golden brown. Serve with hot custard.

Also try

- The world's your oyster on the fruit front, tinned or fresh: peaches, cherries, pears, nectarines, pineapple, banana…

Baked apples with fruit and nuts

This is another dish that brings back memories of childhood. Baked apples always seem to be popular, especially when served with thick cream or ice-cream.

Serves 4

4 large Bramley cooking apples
125g (4½oz) dark muscovado
 sugar
4 tbsp sweet mincemeat
55g (2oz) flaked almonds or
 chopped pecans
1 tsp ground cinnamon
2 tbsp raisins
25g (1oz) unsalted butter
apple juice for basting

1 Preheat the oven to 190°C/375°F/gas mark 5.

2 Remove the cores of the apples, leaving 5mm (¼ inch) at the bottom. Run the tip of a sharp knife round the apple's circumference, just to pierce the skin ½cm (¼ inch) deep. This stops the apples bursting during cooking.

3 Combine the remaining ingredients, except the butter and apple juice, and spoon into the cavities of the apples. Place any excess mixture in the bottom of a buttered baking dish. Place the apples on the fruit, dot the top with butter and bake in the oven for 45 minutes to an hour.

4 Every 10 minutes, add 2 tbsp of apple juice to the bottom of the dish and spoon the juices over the apples. This stops a nasty burnt caramel building up on the bottom of the baking dish.

5 Serve piping hot with double or clotted cream.

Also try

- Substitute thick honey for the sugar.

- Use other dried fruits – cherries, blueberries, cranberries – instead of the mincemeat.

 Apple snow

My Gran had an orchard of old apple varieties, and this pud featured regularly when I was a child, as did everything appley. Do not serve raw eggs to very young children.

Serves 4

6 Bramley apples, peeled, cored and sliced

½ tsp ground cinnamon

5 tbsp caster sugar

125ml (4fl oz) double cream, whipped to soft peaks

3 free-range egg whites

a few toasted almonds (optional)

1 Cook the apples in a little water, together with the cinnamon and enough sugar to sweeten – about 2 tbsp – until soft.

2 When ready, pass through a sieve and allow to cool.

3 Fold the whipped double cream into the apples. Whisk the egg whites to soft peaks, then add the remaining sugar and whisk until they stand up.

4 Fold the egg whites into the apple snow. Sprinkle with toasted almonds or ground cinnamon if you wish and serve with shortbread.

Also try

- Substitute pears or tinned peaches for apples.

● Sponge pudding

Every child enjoys a good sponge pudding. This is the classic recipe, a formula that has been used for years, but it's all but disappeared as we've slipped into the habit of using puddings in supermarket cartons. It's so easy to make though, and the preparation takes very little time. It can either be baked, if you are in a hurry, or steamed if you want it to be a little lighter. If you know the basic recipe, a whole host of different flavours can come into play (see below).

Serves 6-8

4 tbsp of your favourite jam
115g (4oz) unsalted butter, softened (plus extra for greasing)
115g (4oz) caster sugar
2 free-range eggs, beaten
½ tsp vanilla extract
115g (4oz) self-raising flour
a pinch of salt

1   Preheat the oven to 180°C/350°F/gas mark 4, if baking. Grease an 850ml (1½ pint) pudding basin with extra butter and place your jam etc in the bottom (see below).

2   Beat together the butter and sugar until pale and fluffy. Beat the eggs with the vanilla, then gradually fold them into the butter mix, beating continuously until combined. Sift the flour and salt together then, with a light touch, fold into the butter mix. Spoon into the pudding basin.

3   To bake: cook in the preheated oven for 30 minutes, until risen and golden. To steam: cover the basin with a double thickness of greaseproof paper, with a 2.5cm (1 inch) pleat across the centre. Tie with string. Put in the top of a steamer or in a saucepan with an upturned saucer in the bottom and water three-quarters of the way up the sides of the basin. Cover with a lid and steam over a moderate heat for 1¾ hours, checking on the water level from time to time. If it needs topping up, use boiling water.

4   Remove the paper and turn out carefully on to a warm serving dish. Serve with custard or pouring cream.

Also try

● Replace the jam with the same amount of golden syrup, or honey or lemon curd.

● Omit the jam and serve the pudding with chocolate sauce. If you're doing this, replace 25g (1oz) of the flour with 25g (1oz) cocoa powder. Fold in some chocolate chips.

Extra fruity bread pudding

Bread and butter pudding is lovely, but there are ways to make it even more delicious. This one avoids the butter, but manages to be even scrummier than the classic. It's just as good eaten the next day at room temperature.

Serves 6-8

Fruit

175g (6oz) each dried apricots, dried apples and dried pears, roughly chopped

55g (2oz) dried blueberries

225g (8oz) caster sugar

Pudding

8 free-range egg yolks

85g (3oz) caster sugar

450ml (16fl oz) semi-skimmed milk

450ml (16fl oz) double cream

finely grated zest of 1 unwaxed orange and 1 unwaxed lemon

1 tsp vanilla extract

1 tsp orange-blossom water (optional)

a pinch of freshly grated nutmeg

approx. 450g (1lb) brioche or day-old country white bread, crusts removed, cut in 1cm (½ inch) cubes

apricot jam to finish

1 Simmer the fruits in 300ml (10fl oz) water mixed with 115g (4oz) of the caster sugar for about 15 minutes, covered, turning the fruits over from time to time. Drain the fruits and retain the liquid.

2 Place the cooking liquid in a saucepan and make it up to 300ml (10fl oz) with water. Add the remaining sugar. Boil the mixture until it begins to turn golden. Brush the sides of the pan just above the syrup level with water to prevent the sugar crystallizing. Boil until the sugar becomes deep golden but not too dark. Pour the caramel syrup into the bottom of a 2.25 litre (4 pint) gratin dish.

3 Meanwhile, whisk the yolks with the sugar until pale and frothy. Carefully whisk in the milk and cream, then fold in the citrus zests, vanilla, orange-blossom water and nutmeg.

4 Mix together the bread and poached fruit and scatter them over the caramel in the gratin dish. Pour over the cream mix and allow to stand for at least 1 hour, or preferably overnight. This helps 'soufflé' the pudding when it is cooked. Preheat the oven to 180°C/350°F/gas mark 4.

5 Place the gratin dish in a water bath or bain-marie and cook in the oven until nicely browned, about 1¼ hours. Halfway through cooking, dot the top with teaspoons of apricot jam.

Also try

- Use different dried fruits: there's nowt wrong with good old-fashioned sultanas and raisins.

Getting kids cooking

As an adolescent, I went to domestic cookery lessons while on my holidays. I was the only boy in the class, and my family and friends thought that I was a bit of a sissy. I persisted, telling myself that my mates were missing out; I was, after all, in a class full of adolescent girls!

When I decided I wanted to be a chef, my grandmother (who was a bit posh and who had paid my school fees) was horrified. 'Darling,' she said, 'people downstairs cook, gentlemen don't.' Again I persisted and she eventually accepted that she couldn't change my mind. I just loved to cook.

These days, with the proliferation of TV cookery shows, you'd have thought more children would be cooking. Having visited several schools, I know they want to; they love shows such as *Ready Steady Cook,* and Jamie Oliver has made it cool to cook.

The big problem is that not many schools teach cookery any more. They have a subject called 'Food Technology', which has little or no relevance to home cooking. The Government must put cooking back on the curriculum if we are to improve the nation's health. Every child leaving school should know the basics of cookery. In Britain we have some of the best restaurants in the world, but for how much longer? Where is the next generation of cooks going to come from?

It's not just about schools and government, it's about parents too. A child will not learn about good food if all he or she eats is junk food, takeaways, ready-meals, instant canned foods or even fish fingers. Push-button cookery is not the way forward. But how do we get our children to cook? There is no simple answer. I encourage them by rearing and growing food – we have chickens, pigs, ducks, guinea fowl and an abundant garden of vegetables, herbs, salad foods and fruits. They see it grow so they want to cook it.

Letting kids watch cookery shows on TV builds their enthusiasm, but you must extend this into the kitchen. Be prepared for a bomb site at first, it's part of the fun. Don't just teach them about cakes – fairy cakes are all very well, but hundreds and thousands and coloured icing are not the way forward!

Encouragement, not chastisement, is the trick. Buy them some of their own kit: some utensils and a jazzy apron. Make them feel important and useful. You'll be amazed by how quickly they get into it, and they love taking foods to school to give to their friends. Start simple, repetition *is* important at an early age, until the skills are ingrained in their memory banks. Then move on to more complicated cooking, such as sauces and knife skills (you should always be with them when they use knives). Persist, you'll soon make great cooks out of them, and the beauty is that whatever they cook they'll want to eat – although at first *you* may not find it quite so delicious!

'Whatever kids cook they'll want to eat.'

Poached apricots with honey and Greek yoghurt

A healthy pudding, which could be made less healthy but more delicious with a scoop or two of vanilla ice-cream.

Serves 4-6

450g (1lb) dried apricots (ideally
   organic) soaked in 600ml
   (1 pint) apple juice
55g (2oz) caster sugar
4 cardamom pods, crushed
2 tsp fresh lemon juice
4 tbsp thick honey
300ml (10fl oz) very thick Greek
   yoghurt
55g (2oz) flaked almonds, toasted

1   Preheat the oven to 180°C/350°F/gas mark 4.

2   Place the apricots with the apple juice in an ovenproof pan with the sugar, cardamom seeds and lemon juice. Bring to the boil, and then cover with wet parchment paper, put the lid on the pan and cook in the preheated oven for 1 hour.

3   Remove the pan from the oven and allow the apricots to cool in their syrup.

4   To serve, remove the apricots and drain. Open each one and put 1 tsp honey and 1 tsp Greek yoghurt inside it. Top with toasted flaked almonds. Pour some syrup over the apricots.

Also try

- This poaching liquor is good for many other fruits, such as pears, peaches and nectarines

Baked 'souffle' bananas

So simple but often in demand, these bananas – when cooked in their skins – become light and fluffy and a dream to eat.

Serves 4

4 large bananas
4 tbsp Greek yoghurt
1 tbsp runny honey
¼ tsp ground cinnamon
2 tbsp dark muscovado sugar

1   Preheat the oven to 200°C/400°F/gas mark 6. Cook the unpeeled bananas on a baking sheet in the oven until blackened and soft, about 20-30 minutes.

2   Combine the yoghurt, honey and cinnamon. With the tip of a sharp knife, make a skin-deep incision the length of the banana, then pull open the skin to reveal the souffléed banana.

3   Trickle the yoghurt mix the full length of each opened banana, then sprinkle with the sugar. Put a banana in its skin on each of 4 plates and eat while still hot. Beware, as the bananas get exceptionally hot.

Chocolate banana custard

Here's a quick pud that combines flavours all children seem to enjoy.

Serves 4

115g (4oz) plain (semi-sweet)
   chocolate, broken into pieces
300ml (10fl oz) fresh custard
   (bought or home-made)
2 bananas

1   Put the chocolate in a heatproof bowl. Melt the chocolate in the microwave on high power for 1-2 minutes or place the bowl over a pan of gently simmering water and leave until melted. Stir, then set aside to cool.

2   Pour the custard into a bowl and gently fold in the melted chocolate to make a rippled effect. Peel and slice the bananas into the mixture.

3   Spoon the mixture into 4 glasses, and chill for 30 minutes to 1 hour before serving.

Lemon mousse with fresh raspberries

Mousses, apart from chocolate, have slipped out of fashion. There's no particular reason for this, but I think they were considered to be too domestic for the average chef, while at home we have tended to get a little lazy about constructing a pud. I love this lemon mousse for its tangy smoothness. Do not serve raw eggs to young children.

Serves 4

4 free-range eggs
175g (6oz) caster sugar
juice of 3 unwaxed lemons, and
   the finely grated zest of 2
15g (½oz) powdered gelatine
   (1 packet)
200ml (7fl oz) double cream
150ml (5fl oz) pouring cream
225g (8oz) fresh raspberries
icing sugar for dusting

1   Beat the eggs with the sugar until thick, pale and fluffy.

2   Heat the lemon juice and pour into a small bowl. Sprinkle the gelatine on to the hot juice, stir briskly until thoroughly dissolved, then allow to cool slightly. Fold the gelatine liquid into the egg mixture along with the lemon zest.

3   Whip the double cream to soft peaks and fold into the egg, gelatine and juice mixture. Pour into glasses and leave to set in the refrigerator for a couple of hours.

4   Tip some pouring cream on top of each mousse, then arrange the raspberries decoratively. Dust with icing sugar before serving.

Also try

- Use other citrus juices, such as red grapefruit, orange or lime instead of lemon.

Raspberry pavlova roulade

This is not an everyday pud as it's so rich and sweet, but it's so delicious that I had to add it to the book for the odd occasion.

Serves 8

Roulade
9 free-range egg whites
a pinch of salt
375g (13oz) caster sugar
1 tsp cornflour
a pinch of cream of tartar
1 tsp white wine vinegar
2 drops vanilla extract

Filling
600ml (1 pint) double cream (you may not need all of it)
1 jar of your favourite raspberry jam
450g (1lb) fresh raspberries

Raspberry sauce
450g (1lb) fresh raspberries
2 tbsp lemon juice
3 tbsp icing sugar

1   Preheat the oven to 180°C/350°F/gas mark 4. Line a Swiss roll tin or a similar-sized baking tray with greaseproof paper.

2   Whisk the egg whites with the salt in a very clean bowl until soft peaks form. Continue whisking, while adding the sugar, until stiff and shiny. Sprinkle over the cornflour, cream of tartar, vinegar and vanilla and fold in gently.

3   Spread the egg white mix all over the greaseproof paper-lined tray. Flatten the top and smooth the sides.

4   Place in the oven and immediately reduce the heat to 150°C/300°F/gas mark 2. Cook for 20 minutes. Turn off the oven, leave the door slightly ajar and allow to cool. Invert the roulade on to a sheet of greaseproof paper and set aside.

5   Meanwhile, make the filling. Whip the double cream until soft peaks form, cover and refrigerate until needed.

6   For the sauce, put the raspberries in a blender, add the lemon and sugar, and whiz until smooth. Sieve, then refrigerate.

7   To construct the roulade, spread a layer of raspberry jam over the cooled roulade, top with cream and sprinkle with most of the fresh raspberries. Carefully roll up into a roulade.

8   To serve, cut into slices, pour some sauce over and around the roulade, and scatter over the rest of the raspberries.

Also try

- Diced peaches, almonds and Amaretti cream (simply whipped cream flavoured with an almond liqueur).

- Lemon curd, orange pieces and Grand Marnier cream (as above).

- Chocolate spread, cream and sliced bananas.

Raspberry yoghurt crunch

So easy but enjoyable, and it could be eaten at breakfast.

Serves 4

75g (2¾oz) crunchy oat cereal
600g (1lb 5oz) Greek yoghurt
250g (9oz) fresh raspberries

1   Preheat the grill to high. Spread the oat cereal on a baking sheet and place under the hot grill for 3-4 minutes, stirring regularly. Set aside to cool.

2   When the cereal has cooled completely, fold it into the Greek yoghurt, then gently fold in 200g (7oz) of the raspberries, being careful not to crush the berries too much.

3   Spoon the yoghurt mixture into 4 serving glasses or dishes, top with the remaining raspberries and serve immediately.

Summer berry frozen yoghurt

I made this dish on Saturday Kitchen, and for something so simple, the positive response was amazing.

Serves 6

350g (12oz) frozen summer fruits
200g (7oz) Greek yoghurt
25g (1oz) icing sugar
115g (4oz) strawberry jam

1   Put all the ingredients into a food processor and process until combined but still quite chunky. Spoon the mixture into clingfilm-lined 6 x 150ml (5fl oz) ramekin dishes.

2   Cover each dish with more clingfilm and place in the freezer for about 2 hours, or until firm.

3   To turn out the frozen yoghurts, loosen by lifting the clingfilm lining and invert them on to small serving plates. Remove the clingfilm.

4   Allow to sit at room temperature for 10 minutes before serving.

● Summer pudding

A luscious, traditional favourite that makes the most of summer berries and currants. The liqueur can be left out for kids.

Serves 6-8

900g (2lb) raspberries

225g (8oz) redcurrants, picked from the stalks

115g (4oz) blackcurrants, picked from the stalks

225g (8oz) caster sugar

about 8 slices of day-old bread, crusts removed

125ml (4fl oz) Framboise liqueur or Kirsch (optional)

1 Sprinkle the fruits with the sugar and toss gently to combine. Cover and leave to macerate for 2 hours. During this time, the fruit will release lots of juice.

2 Meanwhile line a 1.7 litre (3 pint) pudding basin with clingfilm, then with slices of bread, dipped in juices from the fruit. Make sure the bread overlaps slightly and covers the sides and bottom completely.

3 Tip the fruit and any remaining juices into a non-reactive saucepan with the liqueur, if using, and cook over a medium heat for 4 minutes to release more juices.

4 Using a slotted spoon, fill up the bread-lined basin with fruit. Pour over half the juices, then cover the fruit completely with more bread slices. Reserve the remaining juices. Cover with clingfilm, then top with a plate that fits into the rim of the bowl. Place a heavy weight on top of the plate and refrigerate overnight.

5 When ready to serve, invert the bowl on to a shallow, but not flat dish, and remove the bowl and clingfilm. Serve wedges of the pudding with clotted cream, a few loose berries of your choice, and a little extra of the retained juice.

Also try

- Make an autumn pudding with caramelized apples (see page 12) and blackberries.

Cakes and biscuits

Gone are the days when there was always a cake tin in the larder ready for those hungrier times when the kids would come home from school or run into the house from playing in the garden. Sadly, my mum was useless at making cakes; they usually had the consistency of large biscuits. But my great aunt was a whiz at it – everything, from her lardy cake to her Victoria sponge, had the perfect light touch.

Tea-time was once a treasured part of British society, a pleasant sit-down affair with tea out of bone china rather than big mugs. There would always be sandwiches or bread and jam, a selection of biscuits and a cake or sometimes two. It would last precisely half an hour, an old-fashioned value that unfortunately has limited appeal in the speed of our modern world.

I always used to dread making cakes and biscuits, which was probably the fall-out from my mother's baking! But once you really put your mind to it, they rarely go wrong. Funnily enough, I've learnt more from the lady I call 'mum' on my BBC2 show *Saturday Kitchen*, Mary Berry, who has some wonderful tips.

In this chapter, I've chosen an easy selection of cakes and biscuits that can be knocked up in a hurry even by the most stressed of mums and dads. And it's in the cakes and biscuits department that children can really get involved. They just love all that mixing and messing. Yes, the kitchen counter could end up looking like a bit of a bomb-site, but hey, it's a start and a lovely way of getting them involved in the family cooking.

Remember that most of the recipes in this section are only for moderate use, not for every day – more Sunday than Monday. Children today eat too many sugary foods so, as a rule, when we make cakes in our house they are fruit-based, as this reduces the need for added sugar in the recipe. However, you will get a huge amount of satisfaction once you've made your choice and presented the finished cake to the children: the rewards to the parents will be a feel-good factor on both sides.

'As a rule, when we make cakes they are fruit-based, as this reduces the need for added sugar in the recipe.'

● Orange and almond cake

Cakes are not my forte, but when I discovered this one in Spain, I was over the moon because it is so easy, so delicious and doesn't use any flour.

Serves 8-10

butter, for greasing
4 large navel oranges
200g (7oz) caster sugar
200g (7oz) ground almonds
1 tsp baking powder
6 free-range eggs
juice of ½ lemon

1   Preheat the oven to 190°C/375°F/gas mark 5. Grease and line the base of a 20cm (8 inch) springform cake tin with parchment paper.

2   Put the oranges in a pan and cover with cold water. Cover, bring to the boil, turn down the heat and simmer for 2 hours. Check the water to ensure they don't boil dry. Remove from the heat and leave to cool. This can be done in advance and stored in the refrigerator until you are ready to construct the cake.

3   Remove the oranges from the water, cut 2 of them into chunks and remove any pips. Thinly slice the remaining oranges and lay half of these on the bottom of your cake tin (keep the remaining slices for the top.)

4   Place the chunks of orange in a food processor with all of the remaining ingredients and blitz until mixed.

5   Spoon the mixture into the cake tin. Top with the remaining sliced oranges and bake in the preheated oven for 45 minutes. Keep a careful eye on this – you may need to reduce the temperature, depending on your oven. The cake will be soft and moist, and the usual dry knife test won't work here.

6   Let the cake cool slightly before removing from the cake tin, then leave to cool on a wire rack.

Also try

- Use mashed bananas instead of oranges, but don't cook them.

- Coeliacs should use gluten-free baking powder.

Pear and cranberry upside-down cake

A lovely cake that is always greedily received. When I was young, my grandmother always had a cake ready for tea. Nowadays tea-time has all but disappeared, and where there is a lack of daily exercise that is probably no bad thing. But from time to time, probably at weekends, treat yourself to a little tradition.

Serves 8

125g (4½oz) unsalted butter, at
   room temperature
225g (8oz) caster sugar
1 tsp vanilla extract
2 free-range eggs, separated
325g (11½oz) plain flour
2 tsp baking powder
a pinch of salt
125ml (4fl oz) semi-skimmed milk
¼ tsp cream of tartar

Topping
55g (2oz) unsalted butter
175g (6oz) dark moscovado sugar
2 Williams pears, peeled, cored,
   halved and each sliced into 4
225g (8oz) fresh or frozen
   cranberries

To serve
Greek yoghurt
Runny honey

1. Preheat the oven to 180°C/350°F/gas mark 4. For the topping, put the butter and sugar in a saucepan over a low heat and stir until they melt and come together to make a caramel sauce. Pour into the bottom of a 23cm (9 inch) cake tin and swirl to coat the bottom. Arrange the pear slices, stalk end towards the centre of the tin, all around the tin. In the hole of each slice (created by removing the core) place a few cranberries, then dot them around to fill any gaps.

2. With an electric hand whisk, beat together the butter and caster sugar until pale and fluffy, about 3 minutes. Beat in the vanilla and yolks, one at a time, making sure the butter is incorporated. Sift the flour, baking powder and salt on to the butter mix, alternating with a little milk, and beat.

3. Whisk the egg whites with the cream of tartar until they form soft peaks. Mix a spoonful of the whites into the cake mix to slacken it. Fold in the remainder and combine gently.

4. Pour the cake mix on top of the pears, spreading it evenly. Bake in the middle of the preheated oven for 35 minutes, until golden and the sides are starting to come away from the tin. Allow to cool for 15 minutes before turning out on to a wire rack. Serve with Greek yoghurt and drizzle with honey.

Also try

Instead of pears, try:

- Tinned or fresh peeled peach or nectarine halves, filling the hole with cranberries;

- Plums, halved, stoned and put cut-side down in the caramel.

Easy chocolate cake

A good one for emergencies. Make 2 cakes and sandwich raspberry jam between them, or simply serve with a dusting of icing sugar.

Serves 8

225g (8oz) best-quality dark chocolate (70% cocoa solids), broken into small pieces
3 tbsp semi-skimmed milk
3 tbsp double cream
100g (3½oz) unsalted butter, cut into small cubes
4 free-range eggs, separated
175g (6oz) caster sugar
55g (2oz) plain flour
1 tbsp cocoa powder
1½ tsp baking powder
a pinch of cream of tartar

1   Preheat the oven to 180°C/350°F/gas mark 4. Lightly butter and flour a 23cm (9 inch) springform cake tin and cut a circle of parchment paper to fit the bottom.

2   Place the chocolate in a bowl with the milk, cream and butter and set it over a saucepan of simmering water: the water must not touch the bottom of the bowl. When the chocolate has melted, stir the mixture to bring everything together. Remove from the heat.

3   Meanwhile, beat the egg yolks and sugar together until pale and fluffy. Quickly fold the chocolate mix into the eggs, then sift in the flour, cocoa powder and baking powder.

4   In a very clean bowl, whisk the egg whites with the cream of tartar until they form soft peaks. Mix a spoonful into the cake batter to slacken the mixture, then fold in the remainder until well combined.

5   Pour the batter into the cake tin and bake in the preheated oven for 35-40 minutes, or until a skewer inserted comes out clean. Allow to cool for 15 minutes before turning out on to a cooling rack. The cake will drop slightly in the centre.

Also try

- Add a few white, dark and milk chocolate chips to the mix.

● Carrot and pineapple cake

A light-textured cake loved by all, based on the everyday carrot cake.

Serves 8-10

350g (12oz) wholemeal self-
  raising flour
2 tsp baking powder
½ tbsp ground cinnamon
½ tsp each of freshly ground
  nutmeg and ground allspice
115g (4oz) dark muscovado sugar
125ml (4fl oz) light olive oil
2 free-range eggs, lightly beaten
350g (12oz) carrot, grated
55g (2oz) walnut pieces
115g (4oz) raisins
25g (1oz) desiccated coconut
250g (9oz) canned crushed
  pineapple in natural juice,
  drained

Frosting
140g (5oz) cream cheese or
  mascarpone cheese
250g (9oz) golden icing sugar,
  sifted

1 Preheat the oven to 180°C/350°F/gas mark 4. Grease and base-line a 23cm (9 inch) springform cake tin.

2 Mix all the ingredients together in a large bowl until they are evenly combined.

3 Transfer the mixture to the prepared tin and level the surface. Cook in the centre of the preheated oven for 50-60 minutes, until risen and golden and a fine metal skewer comes out clean when inserted in the cake. Cool in the tin for 15 minutes, then transfer to a wire rack until cold.

4 To make the frosting, in a food processor or by hand, blend together the cream cheese or mascarpone with the golden icing sugar. Spread the frosting over the cake and serve.

Also try

- Use hazelnuts or almonds instead of walnuts.

- Add some pieces of dried fruit, such as sultanas or cherries etc.

● Spiced oat biscuits

A textured biscuit that is not crisp, but provides a savoury nibble.

Makes about 12

85g (3oz) wholemeal flour
½ tsp salt
55g (2oz) porridge oats
½ tsp bicarbonate of soda
½ tsp ground mixed spice
85g (3oz) unsalted butter,
  softened
55g (2oz) apple sauce (from a jar)

1   Preheat the oven to 190°C/375°F/gas mark 5. Grease 2 baking sheets and lightly dust them with flour.

2   Sift the flour and salt into a bowl, tipping in any wholemeal flakes that get left in the sieve. Stir in the oats, bicarbonate of soda and mixed spice.

3   Cream the butter in a separate large bowl until light and fluffy, then fold in the apple sauce a little at a time. Fold in the oat mixture until well combined.

4   Place walnut-sized portions of the biscuit mixture on to the prepared baking sheets, leaving a 5cm (2 inch) space around each one, and then flatten each one slightly with a fork. Bake in the preheated oven for 15 minutes, or until they are beginning to turn golden brown.

5   Remove from the oven and leave to cool completely on the baking sheets, then store in an airtight container until ready to eat.

Also try

- Add some dried fruit – sultanas, dried cherries, blueberries, cranberries.

● Refrigerator biscuits

This is the easiest, quickest biscuit mix in the world and is always useful as a standby.

Makes 18

350g (12oz) self-raising flour
200g (7oz) unsalted butter,
    softened
175g (6oz) light muscovado sugar
½ tsp vanilla extract
1 free-range egg
55g (2oz) chopped dates
25g (1oz) raisins
25g (1oz) dried blueberries

1   Preheat the oven to 180°C/350°F/gas mark 4.

2   Sift the flour into a bowl and set aside.

3   Cream the butter, sugar and vanilla in a separate bowl, then beat in the egg. Add the flour and stir to combine. Finally, fold in the fruit.

4   Make into individual rolls about 4cm (1½ inches) in diameter, wrap in clingfilm and place in the fridge until quite firm. You can keep this 'dough' in the fridge for up to 2 weeks, covered in clingfilm.

5   When ready to cook, slice thinly, approximately 1cm (½ inch) thick, and place the circles on a lightly greased baking tray. Bake in the preheated oven for 10-15 minutes. Remove from the oven, rest for 5 minutes, then remove to a cooling rack and leave until cold. Store in an airtight container.

Also try

● You can change the dried fruit for any type you fancy and/or add a few chopped nuts.

Chocolate chip cookies

This is a simple, foolproof version of a classic American favourite. The children enjoy making these, and that usually means cooking a second batch!

Makes 18

115g (4oz) unsalted butter, softened
75g (2¾oz) caster sugar
75g (2¾oz) dark muscovado sugar
1 free-range egg, lightly beaten
½ tsp vanilla extract
140g (5oz) plain flour
1 tsp bicarbonate of soda
a pinch of salt
finely grated zest of 1 unwaxed orange
85g (3oz) dark or milk chocolate chips
85g (3oz) white chocolate chips

1 Preheat the oven to 190°C/375°F/gas mark 5. Butter and flour a non-stick or ordinary flat baking sheet.

2 Beat the butter with the 2 sugars in a mixing bowl until light and fluffy.

3 Beat the egg and vanilla into the butter mix until combined, then sift in the flour, bicarbonate of soda and salt, a little at a time, mixing well between additions.

4 Next, fold in the orange zest and all the chocolate chips. Mix well until evenly distributed.

5 Spoon small mounds of the mixture on to the prepared baking sheet, leaving 7.5cm (3 inches) between each mound to allow for spreading. You may have to cook them in batches, depending on how many baking trays you have.

6 Bake them in the preheated oven for 12 minutes, until they are an even golden colour. Leave for 1 minute, then transfer to a wire cooling rack. When completely cool, store in an airtight container.

Also try

- A little cocoa powder folded into the flour makes the cookies more chocolatey.

- Omit the orange zest if desired.

● Spiced cats' tongues

A traditional recipe for a biscuits that we used to have at school, known in the French vernacular as *langues du chat*. Perfect to accompany ice-cream or as a nibble with a cup of tea.

Makes 20-25 biscuits

55g (2oz) unsalted butter, softened
70g (2½oz) caster sugar
2 free-range egg whites, at room temperature
45g (1¾oz) plain flour
¼ tsp salt
¼ tsp ground cinnamon
¼ tsp powdered ginger

1   Preheat the oven to 180°C/350°F/gas mark 4. Line baking trays with parchment paper.

2   Beat the butter and sugar together using an electric hand-whisk until pale and fluffy.

3   Fold in the egg whites until combined, then sift in the flour, salt and spices. Beat until smooth, then refrigerate for half an hour.

4   Spread individual biscuits, using a palette knife or the back of a spoon, on to the parchment paper-lined trays. They must be very thin and should be rectangular, about 2.5 x 7.5cm (1 x 3 inches).

5   Bake in the preheated oven until golden, about 8-10 minutes. Leave for 1 minute then lift them carefully onto a wire cooking rack. When completely cool, store in an airtight container.

Also try

- While the biscuits are still warm, mould them into different shapes, wrap them around a little oiled plastic round-handled spoon, or twist them at each end to create a spiral.

Celebrations

Whether you're hosting a children's parties or an adult party that your children are attending, the trick is to serve food that is compatible to both age groups. I admit to cringing when I see the food dished out for my children at the numerous parties they attend, usually at the ice-rink, swimming pool or theme park.

Do we have to stoop to the lowest common denominator? I don't think so. Caterers need to change their attitudes towards children. I often find them so patronising in their assumption that children only want what they see on the TV. It's time to put dishes on the menu that both kids and adults will enjoy; half-portions are all that is needed.

Most children will eat chicken, steak or even fish if it is filleted, and many adults have a secret yearning for puds such as jelly and custard, with the jelly made with fresh fruit juice of course. There is a fine balance to be achieved. I don't want to turn my children into food bores so I don't think smoked salmon, chicken liver kebabs or even olives are the way forward. But I do find that my children and their friends enjoy Oriental offerings: some spare ribs, saté, prawn or pork patties, all the sort of things that adults enjoy as well.

A celebration means having fun, food should not be forced on children if they are not going to enjoy it. There are times when you may be appalled at the foods your children are eating at their friends' parties, but they are having fun, so grin and bear it.

At a party it's all about balance, something for everyone: food, drink and entertainment. Your party is the one that counts. There will be 15-20 other kids' parties during the year, it's all the rage, every classmate has a birthday, your child will usually be invited, so let them get on with it. But when it's your party, it's your rules, your house, your food. But always remember that chicken nuggets or Turkey Twizzlers don't have to come out of a bag; you can make your own and you'll know what goes into them... it's your call.

'It's time to put dishes on the menu that both kids and adults will enjoy; half-portions are all that is needed.'

Saucy pigs in blankets

An easy finger food that children and adults will both enjoy.

Makes 6

6 favourite pork sausages

4 tsp sweet chilli pickle (e.g.
   Doritos or your favourite brand)

12 rashers rindless smoked
   streaky bacon

1   Preheat the grill to medium.

2   Partially cut the sausages lengthways, making a deep slash.

3   Spoon a little of the pickle into this split, then wrap 2 rashers of the bacon carefully around each sausage, making the filling secure.

4   Place the sausages under the grill for about 15 minutes, turning frequently (and carefully) until the sausages and bacon are cooked through. Serve warm.

Also try

● Use chopped prunes instead of pickle.

Crispy spiced chicken

Chicken with attitude. This dish puts loads of flavour into the children's favourite meat.

Serves 4

3 free-range chicken breast fillets, each cut into strips

2 free-range egg whites, beaten

3 tbsp fine rice flour

1 red chilli, seeded and finely chopped

3 tbsp chopped coriander

4 kaffir lime leaves, very finely chopped

2 tbsp sesame seeds (optional)

½ tsp salt

¼ tsp cayenne pepper

2-3 tbsp vegetable oil

Dipping sauce

3 tbsp soy sauce

2 tbsp lemon juice

1 tbsp light muscovado sugar

1 Combine the chicken, egg whites, rice flour, chilli, coriander, lime leaves, sesame seeds (if using), salt and cayenne in a bowl.

2 Heat a frying pan over medium heat. Add the oil and cook the chicken for 5 minutes on each side, or until golden and cooked through. Drain on kitchen paper.

3 To make the dipping sauce, place the soy, lemon juice and sugar in a bowl and mix to combine.

4 Serve the chicken with the dipping sauce on the side.

Also try

- This marinade works well with beef fillet or pork (grill as strips under a high heat for 2-3 minutes on each size, depending on the thickness of the meat), or even firm-fleshed fish such as swordfish, monkfish or tuna.

Samosas

Samosas are a form of camouflage for vegetables and are always popular at parties.

Makes 30

1 packet frozen filo pastry, thawed, each piece cut in 3
vegetable oil for deep-frying

Filling
3 large potatoes, boiled and coarsely mashed
85g (3oz) frozen peas, thawed
55g (2oz) canned sweetcorn, drained
175g (6oz) baby cauliflower florets, cooked
1 tsp ground coriander
1 tsp ground cumin
1 small onion, finely chopped
2 green chillies, seeded and finely chopped
2 tbsp chopped coriander
2 tbsp chopped mint
salt to taste
juice of 1 lemon

To serve
sweet chilli sauce

1   Toss all the filling ingredients together in a large mixing bowl until they are well blended. Adjust the seasoning with salt and lemon juice, if necessary.

2   Using a single strip of pastry at a time, place 1 tsp of the filling mixture at one end of the strip and diagonally fold the pastry up to form a triangle shape. Damp the ends with water to seal. Use all the filling and pastry to make about 30 samosas.

3   Heat the oil for deep-frying in a large pan. When the oil is hot and slightly smoking, gently drop in as many samosas as will fit easily in one layer. Fry until golden brown and cooked through, turning if necessary – about 4 minutes. Adjust the heat as necessary. Remove with a slotted spoon and drain on a wire rack, then on kitchen paper. Cook the remaining samosas in the same way. Keep them hot while frying the rest. Serve with sweet chilli sauce.

Also try

- Play around with different vegetables.

- Add a little garam masala, curry powder or chilli powder.

Basic pizza base

A basic pizza base to which you can add all sorts of toppings.

Makes 2 x 23cm (9 inch) pizzas or 1 large pizza

1½ tsp active dried yeast
a pinch of caster sugar
50ml (2fl oz) lukewarm water
225g (8oz) plain flour, sifted
125ml (4fl oz) water
¾ tsp salt
3 tbsp olive oil

1   By hand, combine the yeast, sugar, lukewarm water, and 25g (1oz) of the flour in a large bowl. Leave to prove for 10 minutes in a warm place.

2   Add the remaining flour and water, the salt and olive oil, and mix well with a wooden spoon. Turn out on to a work surface and knead for 7-10 minutes, until smooth and elastic. The dough should feel moist to the touch.

3   Place the dough in an oiled bowl and turn to coat the top with oil. Cover with clingfilm and leave to rise in a warm place for 1-1½ hours, until doubled in size.

4   Cut the dough in half or leave whole, depending, on the size of pizza you require. Roll it into 2 x 23cm (9 inch) circles 3-5mm (⅛-¼ inches) thick or 1 large pizza, top with your favourite topping and bake according to the recipe instructions.

Leek, pancetta and goat's cheese pizza

A fairly unusual offering in the pizza stakes.

Makes 2 x 23cm (9 inch) pizzas

2 pizza bases, cold (see above)
extra virgin olive oil
25g (1oz) unsalted butter
300g (10½oz) baby leeks, trimmed,
   or ordinary leeks, sliced thinly
   on the diagonal
salt and ground black pepper
½ tsp soft thyme leaves
150g (5½oz) fresh goat's cheese
55g (2oz) pancetta, cut into
   lardons

1   Preheat the oven to 220°C/425°F/gas mark 7. If you have one, place a pizza stone on the bottom of the oven and heat to max for 1 hour. Heat 1 tbsp of the oil and the butter in a large frying pan. Add the leeks and stew over a low heat for 10-15 minutes, until tender, stirring occasionally. Season generously, then stir in the thyme. Leave to cool a little.

2   Spread the leek mixture over the pizza bases and crumble the goat's cheese on top. Scatter over the pancetta and bake, one at a time, for 12-15 minutes, until the rims are golden. Add a drizzle of olive oil. Serve at once.

Mini ham and egg cups

Jill Dupleix taught me this recipe on *Saturday Kitchen*. We have given it to my children and they have loved it ever since. This is my interpretation.

Makes 12

25g (1oz) unsalted butter
12 very thin slices good-quality
  cooked ham
12 free-range eggs
4 tbsp Greek yoghurt
salt and ground black pepper
4 tbsp freshly grated Parmesan

1   Preheat the oven to 180°C/350°F/gas mark 4. Lightly butter a 12-hole muffin tray.

2   Line the base and sides of each mould with a slice of ham, then break an egg into the hollow.

3   Drizzle with some yoghurt and scatter with salt, pepper and Parmesan.

4   Bake in the preheated oven for 15-20 minutes, until the eggs are just set and starting to shrink away from the sides of the tin. Leave to cool for 5 minutes, then run a knife around each mould to loosen the ham and egg, and remove to a wire tray. Eat warm, or at room temperature.

Also try

- Use good-quality thin smoked bacon instead of ham.

- Place a slice of tomato at the bottom of the ham before cracking the egg.

- Use double cream instead of yoghurt.

● Triple chocolate brownies

Things don't get much better than these brownies, so they should only be eaten on special occasions.

Makes 18

280g (10oz) plain chocolate (70% cocoa solids), broken into pieces

280g (10oz) unsalted butter, diced

175g (6oz) plain flour

1 tsp baking powder

280g (10oz) caster sugar

4 large free-range eggs, lightly beaten

1 tsp vanilla extract

85g (3oz) milk chocolate, broken into 5mm (¼ inch) chunks

85g (3oz) white chocolate, broken into 5mm (¼ inch) chunks

85g (3oz) shelled pecans, broken into pieces and lightly roasted

1   Preheat the oven to 180°C/350°F/gas mark 4. Line a 30 x 20 x 4cm (12 x 8 x 1½ inch) tin with lightly buttered greaseproof paper or foil.

2   Put the plain chocolate and butter in a large heatproof bowl, place over a pan of simmering water and allow to melt. It will look greasy, but don't worry, for as soon as you stir it you will have a wonderful smooth, silky chocolate sauce.

3   Sift the flour and baking powder into a bowl and set aside. Remove the melted chocolate from the heat and stir in the sugar. Add the eggs and vanilla essence. Fold in the flour, milk and white chocolate and nuts.

4   Pour the chocolate mixture into the prepared cake tin. Bake in the preheated oven for 25-30 minutes. The top should be firm but the inside should feel soft when cooked. Allow to cool in the tin.

5   Remove the brownies from the tin, refrigerate, then cut into squares. Serve with vanilla ice-cream or a glass of milk.

Also try

- Add some dried fruit and alternative nuts.

Banana pancakes with chocolate fudge sauce

**Who doesn't love bananas and chocolate –
a classic combination.**

Serves 6

Pancake batter
175g (6oz) plain flour
a pinch of salt
2 tsp caster sugar
2 large free-range eggs and 1 egg
 yolk
150ml (5fl oz) each of milk and
 water, mixed
2 tbsp melted unsalted butter,
 plus extra for cooking the
 pancakes

Filling
115g (4oz) cream cheese
150g (5½oz) Greek yoghurt
2 tbsp runny honey
2 large ripe bananas, peeled and
 finely sliced

Chocolate sauce
115g (4oz) unsalted butter
115g (4oz) light muscovado sugar
25g (1oz) cocoa powder
4 tbsp golden syrup
150ml (5fl oz) single cream

To serve
1-2 bananas (optional)

1   For the pancake batter, sift the flour into a bowl and add the salt and sugar. Add the eggs and yolk and beat to combine. Add the milk and water slowly, and stir until the batter is covered in bubbles. Allow the batter to stand in a cold place for an hour.

2   Add the melted butter to the batter. Heat a little butter in your pancake pan, running it round to coat the sides of the pan. Pour in just enough batter to run over and cover the base. Cook until golden underneath, then turn over with a palette knife and cook for a minute or so longer. Remove from the pan and keep warm while you make the rest of the pancakes using all the batter. You need 12 pancakes.

3   Mix together the cream cheese, yoghurt and honey, and beat until smooth. Carefully fold in the sliced bananas. Divide the filling between the pancakes and carefully roll them up, making sure your filling goes right to the edge of the pancake when rolled up. Allow 2 pancakes per person and arrange on a warmed serving plate.

4   Finally, prepare the chocolate sauce. Beat the butter, sugar and cocoa powder together, then place in a saucepan with the golden syrup and cream. Place on a medium heat and simmer until the sauce comes together.

5   Leave to cool for about 5 minutes, then pour over the pancakes; any sauce left over can be served separately.

6   Serve with extra sliced bananas, if liked.

Also try

- Use poached pears or raspberries instead of the bananas.

Index